HIGH PERFORMANCE
MIDDLE-DISTANCE RUNNING

David Sunderland

Foreword by Frank W. Dick OBE

THE CROWOOD PRESS

First published in 2005 by
The Crowood Press Ltd
Ramsbury, Marlborough
Wiltshire SN8 2HR

www.crowood.com

British Library Cataloguing-in-Publication Data
A catalogue record for this book is available from the British Library.

ISBN 1 86126 756 8

Acknowledgements
The author would like to thank Alison J. Smallman for her help with the
illustrations and diagrams, and Spencer G. Duval for his help with
photographs and editing.

Throughout this book 'he', 'him' and 'his', etc, are used as neutral
pronouns and as such refer to both males and females.

Frontispiece: Poetry in motion – the perfect relaxed technical model.
© Mark Shearman – Athletics Images (athleticsimages@aol.com)

Typeset by NBS Publications, Basingstoke, Hampshire, RG21 5NH

Printed and bound in Great Britain by Biddles Ltd, King's Lynn

Contents

Foreword

It is a real privilege for me to pen the foreword to *High Performance Middle-Distance Running*. Dave Sunderland has been a respected coaching colleague and personal friend for over twenty years. His experience of working with athletes from the young beginner through to the Olympic elite is the very DNA of this book.

He has underpinned his very practical and instantly usable advice with a robust, values-based philosophy, explaining its purpose, principles and practice with immense clarity as he ranges through exercise, progression, training programmes and plans. His teaching and coaching years enrich his treatment of technique, fitness, tactics and attitude. Without doubt, this book is destined to become an essential reference work for the middle-distance athletics coach who is committed to being effective in leading an athlete's pursuit of excellence.

I know that readers will find this book valuable and enjoyable.

Frank W. Dick, OBE

Introduction

Any aspiring coach will be constantly searching for more information and more knowledge which will give him and his athletes the extra edge. Unfortunately, there is a paucity of information on practical field experience available for any aspiring and potentially successful coach. That is why I was pleased to have the opportunity to share my thoughts and experiences and, I hope, go some way towards helping to fill this void. Although it became a labour of love, it was something I wanted to do to help other and like-minded coaches with a thirst for knowledge. It also helped me to crystallize my own views, ideas and philosophy on how a middle-distance runner's season and career should be designed, developed and progressed.

My experiences encompass the whole spectrum of endurance running. I was a national standard athlete who gravitated towards coaching while at college. I was also a co-founding member of the Cannock Chase Athletic Club in 1970. Here my experiences covered coaching in all events and from this I gained an insight into how the training for these could assist my own middle-distance group. In a similar way, I have looked at the training methods used in other endurance sports, such as cycling, swimming, cross-country skiing and rowing, to see how they could be adapted to benefit my own athletes. I became the Midlands middle-distance staff coach, as well as being in charge of coach education for the area.

From here I graduated to National Junior Coach and then to National Senior Coach, a position which I held for over fifteen years and have recently returned to. During this period I was able to witness at first-hand high-performance middle-distance runners. My role as national event coach took me to every major championship as a team coach – the Olympics, the world championships indoors and out, the European championships indoors and out, the Commonwealth Games, the World junior championships, the European junior championships, the world cross-country championships and the European cross-country championships.

On a personal level, I have coached numerous national champions on the track, indoors and at cross-country, and over forty international athletes and medallists at virtually all the major championships. I have also been heavily involved throughout the last thirty years in the development and delivery of the coach education system for UKA. Similarly, for the last twenty years I have been a senior lecturer for the International Amateur Athletic Federation, speaking in over a dozen countries on coach education. Throughout all this time, not only with club athletics but also in my role as county schools secretary and team manager for Staffordshire schools over a thirty-year period, I have constantly been in touch with athletics at the grass-roots level. My range and experience therefore are far-reaching, as regards both personal coaching and also coach education. In both these areas I have past and current experience of the entire range of endurance running, working at all levels of ability up to that of high-performance middle-distance runners on the international and the world stage.

Coaching middle-distance runners requires an understanding of the physiological requirements of the event and the type of training that will produce the desired results in it. It requires good man-management skills, not only with athletes but also in building up and developing support teams. Furthermore it calls for the psychological skills necessary to be able to motivate and lift athletes in order to get the best out of them. A good coaching eye is also essential in order to be able to pick up technical faults, signs of overstraining or any prospective injuries or illness. An ability to plan and develop the progression of an athlete, not only through the season but in his or her career is essential. By using this knowledge, each coach will evolve his own philosophy of coaching. Most have knowledge of and ability in the majority of these areas, but the successful coach is the one who knows how to mix all these requirements together. This involves planning the correct requirements for the correct time of the year and in the correct proportions, successfully applying this knowledge in a yearly plan, and then having the confidence and ability to put it into practice in the training environment and determine how an athlete progresses. This is where coaching becomes an art, one which is nurtured over years of experience, combined with a thirst for knowledge, self-improvement and the willingness never to stop learning and challenging oneself. A coach should be constantly reassessing and re-evaluating himself, his training programmes and his athletes.

This book adopts a practical, common-sense approach which will, I hope, provide the building blocks upon which a successful coaching programme and philosophy may be developed.

CHAPTER 1
The Philosophy of Coaching

INTRODUCTION

All athletes are individuals and must be treated as such in any coaching situation. It is crucially important in relation to their development to make sure that their individual training is progressed slowly through the correct stages and at the correct time of the year. Particular attention and care must be given in the early stages of an athlete's career both to his growth and his physical development. It is quite possible with younger athletes that their biological development progresses more quickly than their chronological age. Here care must be taken with loading, stress levels, the types of surface being used, the recoveries and the level of intensity of the training sessions.

All middle-distance runners throughout the athletic year and throughout their careers should engage in the training process. The training year should have an objective and the year's training plan should reflect this. The plan will then be implemented and the results recorded and evaluated. To achieve this, the process will progress from an individual *training unit* (a particular exercise, such as a 10-mile run, which will take place during one training *session*) through to a group of training units called a *micro-cycle*. This is organized so that the athlete gains the optimum value from each unit. A micro-cycle may vary in length from a week up to a month. Each unit contained in a micro-cycle should have a specific objective, which should change from

unit to unit. Similarly, the amount of the loading and the intensity of the units within the micro-cycle will vary from unit to unit. This process has clear objectives, is planned, implemented, evaluated and then refined. In practice, to get the optimum effect this means ensuring that a low-intensity training unit to aid recovery should always follow a high-intensity training unit. A unit of technique work or a coordination unit may precede an endurance-conditioning unit but should never follow it. This is to ensure that the athlete is fresh and not fatigued when undertaking such specific quality training.

While the micro-cycle leads to varied training units it is also systematic and ordered, leading to the correct and gradual progression required for correct development. The *macro-cycle* is the cumulative effect of repeating the micro-cycles over a given period with a particular objective as the goal. In the preparation phase of the athletic year this would be to lay a good aerobic endurance base in readiness for the more intense and specific work that will follow later in the year. The macro-cycle is sometimes referred to as a block of training or a *meso-cycle*. A macro-cycle should be continued for as long as it takes the athlete to achieve the training objectives or for as long as the athlete can maintain concentration, accept the stresses of the repeated micro-cycles and adapt to the load and intensity of them. With the pre-competition macro-cycle the training intensity should be slowly progressed or kept at the same level, with full recovery between units. The build up to competition should be stress-free and psychologically stimulating, leading to the athlete performing to his peak in the competition.

THE PROCESS OF TRAINING

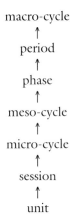

macro-cycle

↑

period

↑

phase

↑

meso-cycle

↑

micro-cycle

↑

session

↑

unit

Three physiological laws affect the middle-distance runner's training unit: the law of overload, the law of specificity and the law of reversibility.

THE LAW OF OVERLOAD

This law means that any improvement in fitness requires a progressively increased training load to challenge the athlete's current fitness level. The training load acts as a stimulus and elicits a response from the athlete's body (Fig. 1). The training loading or intensity causes fatigue and when the training is concluded recovery occurs. If the loading or intensity is correct, after recovery the fitness level will be improved. This overcompensation of the body or training effect is what training is all about. The training units and micro-cycles, if correctly planned and progressed, will result in an improved fitness level when the athlete has

recovered from the training session. However, if the training load is too little the overcompensation after recovery will be less than that required. If the training load is too great, then the athlete will be fortunate to return to the original fitness level (Fig. 2).

THE LAW OF SPECIFICITY

This law means that the training load prescribed for each unit will determine the training effect. The training must be specific to the individual athlete and to the specific demands of the event to realize the desired effect. The training load becomes specific when it has the correct training ratio and structure of loading. This means that in a track repetition session the number of repetitions, their speed and the recovery between them is specific to the athlete's ability. This is so that he is able to achieve the required training effect. The intensity of a training unit is the quality or difficulty of the training load prescribed for that unit. The extent of the training load is the number of repetitions, the time set in which to run the repetitions and the distance of the repetitions. The recovery is the prescribed time between the repetitions. Specificity in training means that it is specific to the athlete, the time of year and his event. Therefore the specific training required for a middle-distance runner will be different to that required for a thrower, a sprinter or a jumper.

THE LAW OF REVERSIBILITY

This law means that fitness levels will fall if the loading is not constantly repeated. The fitness level will revert to where it was before the start of training. If the training is not progressive and more challenging, the athlete's fitness will level off and remain constant. If the training ends, the athlete's

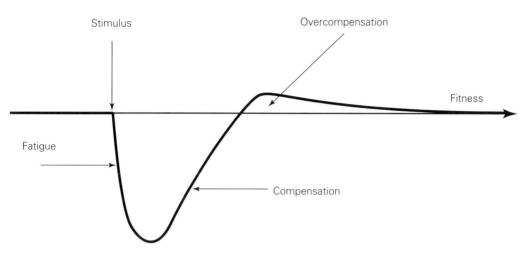

Fig. 1 Through using the standard principle of overload the body is capable of adapting to training loads.
If the loads are correct in their duration, frequency and intensity they cause overcompensation.
If the loads are increased progressively they cause repeated overcompensation and higher levels of adaptation and fitness. Fig.1 shows the correct training level.

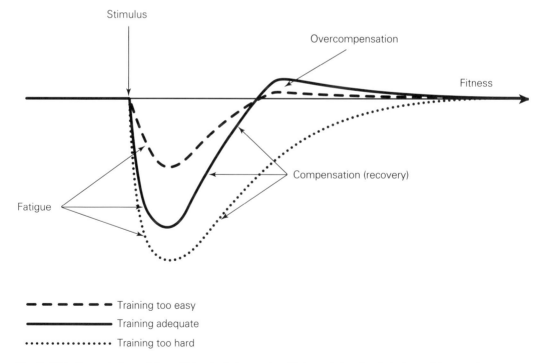

Fig.2. This figure (adapted from Yakovlev) shows that if the training loads or intensities are the same or too far apart there is no increase in the fitness level. Overtraining or incomplete adaptation occurs when training loads are too great or too close to the athlete's fitness level. *Adaptation is specific to the specific nature of the training.*

fitness level will gradually drop until it reaches the level required for normal daily activities. Therefore the training load must continue to increase if the athlete's general and specific fitness is to increase. The load must increase regularly; this is known as *progressive overload* for the performance level to improve. Rest and recuperation are equally as important as the training load itself. If the correct recovery from the high training load is not achieved the training effect will diminish. Active rest, particularly during the transition phase, is also beneficial. This light type of training includes jogging or participation in other sports. It allows the athlete to recover completely while maintaining a general fitness level.

OVERTRAINING

overload (desirable)
↓
overtrain (occasionally)
↓
over-reaching (retrievable)
↓
serious overtraining
(at least 6 months off training)

TRAINING INTENSITY

The athlete's training level or the training intensity of a training unit is divided into three stages. The first is the *immediate training effect*, which, for the middle-distance athlete, is an increase of his heart rate, a build up of lactate and fatigue. The second stage is known as the *residual effect* and is what the immediate effect is turned into through time, until the next repetition or unit. This effect takes place in the recovery phase, after the end of the training session and is the regenerative process. The third and final stage is known as the *cumulative effect*.

This is brought about by the repeated residual effects of the training units in a micro-cycle combined with the correctly timed and progressive training loads.

To know how best to utilize these principles in the training programme, the coach needs to have a good knowledge of the training systems available that will produce these effects. Over the years certain systems and training ideas have been introduced, developed and refined by a great many coaches. Knowing his athlete's strengths and weaknesses, the judicious coach will select and blend into the training programme many of the following methods.

TRAINING METHODS

Fartlek

Fartlek is a Swedish word meaning speed play and was introduced by Gosta Holmer, coach to Gunder Hagg and Arne Anderson. This type of training is done on forest paths over undulating terrain. During a set period the athlete runs as he pleases and as he feels. He will sometimes run hard, sometimes more easily and at others will run fast either on the flat or up a hill. The idea of *fartlek* training is to encourage the athlete to fulfil himself in a natural training environment. In this way he covers many miles and improves both his aerobic base and cardiovascular system. In the track season the *fartlek* sessions are integrated with track work.

Interval Training

In the early 1920s and 1930s the Finnish runner Paavo Nurmi (twenty-two world records and twelve Olympic medals) and his coach Lauri Pikkala used shorter duration training periods with adequate recovery in place of longer, slower endurance running. Without the scientific knowledge now available, they were unknowingly providing training which stimulated a more intense response; coupled with the correct recovery, this type of training equipped Nurmi more easily to meet the demands of his events. This was interval training in its infancy.

Waldemar Gerschler from Germany, coach to Rudolf Harbig and Josy Barthel, in conjunction with a compatriot Dr H. Reindell, was the coach who introduced interval training. In a training unit Gerschler would have a set number of repetitions known as intervals which were run over distances of either 100 or 200m. The set recovery time allowed the athletes to run these repetitions very quickly. This type of training was popularized and developed further in Britain by the Austrian Franz Stampfl, coach to Roger Bannister and Ralph Doubell. Stampfl developed interval training by making the repetition distance much longer and, with his method, the distances ranged from 400m up to distances of 1½ miles. His recovery times were equal to the time of the repetition or longer and the repetitions were run at faster than race pace. Mihaly Igloi, a Hungarian responsible for numerous world record holders and many sub-4min milers, refined interval running even more. With his system the total length of the repetitions run was one-and-a half times to double that of the race distance. For an 800m runner this would mean running 1,200 to 1,600m in total by using interval training. He also halved the recovery times and was the first coach to introduce sets into his athlete's training programmes. For example: 2 × 4 × 600m with a 300m jog between the repetitions and a 600m jog between sets. Emil Zatopek, the great Czechoslovak athlete of the 1950s, took interval training to its extreme with a large number of repetitions and short recoveries between them. Although a long-distance runner himself, he showed the sort of training

which the human body was capable of undertaking. Yuri Suslov, the Soviet coach responsible for his country's successful women middle-distance runners, refined interval running even further. With his method the total of the intervals run was equivalent to the race distance. This allowed the repetitions to be run at faster than the required race pace.

The success of these methods of interval training is that they are precise, easily measured and the progression in training can be seen. The coach can also control the variables involved, the number of repetitions and sets, the speed of the repetitions, the distance of the repetitions and the recovery between them. The recovery phase may be a jogged distance, a set time or a pulse recovery.

Block Training

Other coaches added a different element to middle-distance training. One of these was the New Zealander Arthur Lydiard, coach to Peter Snell and Murray Halberg. Lydiard introduced the system of block training. With this method he would have a ten-week block of marathon training, which systematically progressed to over 100 miles per week. This was followed by a six-week block with the emphasis on uphill running, bounding and downhill running work. The final block of training had a greater emphasis on repetition work, interval training and time trials. As well as being responsible for block training, Lydiard introduced the concept of having an easy day of training after an intense training session and also the idea of athletes' tapering their training to be able to peak for an important competition (*see* Chapter 6).

Total Conditioning

Percy Cerutty, the Australian coach to Herb Elliot, was yet another innovative coach who broadened both the coach's and the athlete's horizons. He believed in running close to nature and so set up a training camp in the dunes near to the sea at Portsea in Australia, using the dunes for resistance work and conditioning training. He was also the coach who developed conditioning even further by introducing weight training into his athlete's training programmes. He made athletes and coaches aware of the importance of diet, but, above all, of how powerful a tool the mind is in both training and competition.

The Oregon System

Bill Bowerman, coach to Steve Prefontaine in Oregon, developed a system referred to as either the 'Oregon system' or the 'Complex system'. This worked on a monthly cycle and each schedule was specific to the individual athlete. He believed in the optimum amount of work, incorporated with the optimum blend of different types of work. This meant that he would, throughout the cycle, include each week a long run, a *fartlek* session, steady runs, plus two track sessions both of which had goal times set for each month. The times were achieved by varying the number of sets, repetitions and recoveries so that the maximum number of repetitions, with the shortest possible recovery time, could be run at the set goal pace by the end of the month (*see* Chapter 6). Once this was achieved, the goal pace for the next month was reduced.

Long, Steady Distance

Ernst Van Aaken, from Germany, pioneered long, steady distance running, sometimes referred to as LSD. He believed that most athletes could run reasonably quickly but did not have the endurance base to continue to run for any length of time. To achieve a large endurance base he advocated large amounts of steady-state running with heart rates around 130, interspersed with speed

runs. His training ratio was 35 miles of steady running to 1 mile of speed running. He also believed that the key to achieving this high steady-state running mileage was to reduce the athlete's body weight to below the norm. His most successful exponent of this system was Harald Norpoth. But the danger with this type of training is that it can lead to anorexia, particularly in young female athletes. If done correctly, however, with the added use of vitamin supplements, the incidence of injury is very low.

Five-pace System

In Britain some coaches tend to favour the five-pace system of training. With this method the repetitive sessions are done at 5,000m-, 3,000m-, 1,500m-, 800m- or 400m-pace. The idea is to give the athlete over-distance endurance through the 5,000- and the 3,000m-pace repetition, under-distance speed through the 800- and the 400m-pace repetition, while still training for his event-specific race distance, the 1,500m. The five different paces are rotated so that over-distance work, event-specific work and under-distance work can all be covered. This method, favoured by Sebastian Coe among others, is explained along with some other systems in Chapter 6.

SUMMARY

From this variety of training systems a coach will choose the ones which are best suited to the needs of his athlete and blend them judiciously into a successful training programme that caters for the athlete's requirements. To do this successfully he must understand when and where to use the methods and what are the effects of a particular type of training. As well as having this knowledge, the good coach also has to have expertise in many other areas.

Possibly the key one is his interpersonal skills with his athletes and the relationship he builds up with each of them. He has to demonstrate integrity in case the athlete is undergoing personal or emotional problems. He should be fair and impartial so that each athlete receives individual attention. His role will undoubtedly differ from athlete to athlete, he will often become a surrogate father to the younger ones and a confidant to his more mature ones who are having personal or emotional problems. Therefore he needs to be a good listener as well as a good motivator. He must get to know his athletes, not just in an athletic sense, but also know what their home backgrounds and personal situations are like. This will also give him an insight into the ambition of each athlete and an appreciation of what he is trying to achieve.

The coach should be perceptive and be able to pick up the mood swings of his athletes. He should also be totally honest with them so that they know where they stand and are not led to believe they are capable of more than their abilities will allow. He should also be loyal to them, and through this, and his honesty, he should in return expect to earn their trust, loyalty and respect. The coach should also look and act the part, he should be well presented, punctual, the constant in the group and act professionally at all times.

As a coach, he must have a great knowledge of the events in which he specializes and a good coaching eye which will enable him both to pick up any problems with technique or stress and alter the training accordingly. He must be able to see the potential of his athlete and develop it to the full. He is also the planner and the controller, not just of the individual training units, but also for the whole year. He therefore must be constantly appraising both himself and his athletes. He should be creative in his coaching, looking for different training environments and different types of training when these are required. No coach is an island and when problems crop up he needs to know where to turn to for advice. Therefore he needs to build up over time a variety of support systems, involving, for example, physiologists, physiotherapists and masseurs. These systems will be discussed in more detail below. With younger athletes he needs to be constantly aware of their biological development as opposed to their assumed chronological development. This means that all their training should be progressed systematically. With older athletes he should take into account how long they have been training and the physical demands on them of their employment. The coach also needs to be a good motivator to get the best out of his athletes. This means using his knowledge of each of his athletes and using a different motivational approach for each. Each athlete has different requirements and different strengths and weaknesses and therefore requires an individual training programme. Nonetheless, whatever motivational method the coach uses he should, above all, inspire his athletes.

Before a race, the coach is there to encourage and reassure. If the training has been going well the athlete will be confident. But if before the race the coach is nervous it will make for a nervous athlete. In this situation he needs to keep well away from his athlete until after the race. He should allow him to become far more self-sufficient in this situation. When the athlete achieves his goal and competes at a major championship it is unlikely that he will have access to his coach in the warm-up area. Therefore the earlier the athlete becomes more self-sufficient the better. If the race goes well the athlete should be praised, but if it does not a candid assessment must be made to come up with the reason for the sub-standard performance. No athlete continually trains hard deliberately to perform badly. Therefore once some time has elapsed to give time for reflection, an assessment of the possible reasons for the poor performance should be made and a solution arrived at and acted upon.

Coaching comes from the experience of working with athletes at all levels. To give each the individual attention he deserves and to ensure that he fulfils his potential, the coach should not dilute his energies and expertise by having a group of more than six to ten athletes. Because time is the most essential commodity a coach has to give an athlete, if the coach has a larger group he will inevitably give less time to each. The experience he gains in the field will show him that if an athlete is running and racing well he does not need to train any harder than he already is. Similarly, if an athlete is training hard but his performances are not reflecting this effort it could mean that he is becoming stale. This may have a number of causes, such as a poor diet, insufficient sleep, too many races, an iron deficiency, fatigue from his daily occupation or emotional stresses. The confidence and self-belief that the coach has gained through his own experience in the field will help him and his athletes to overcome these problems. The athletes will become mirror images of their coach. A positive, confident coach will produce positive, confident athletes.

The coach should leave no factor unexplored in his quest for improvement. Through developing technique mobility and drills he is making his athletes more economical. Through his progressive training programmes, conditioning and the development of the energy pathways he is making his athletes more physiologically efficient. Through his planning and preparation, tactics, motivation and the surrounding support systems he is enabling his athletes to execute this economy and efficiency through their performance in the competitive environment. In essence, *Economy + Efficiency + Execution = Excellence*.

Above all, the coach should be available. He will be the constant in the group, week in, week out, year in, year out. If he is not available and inaccessible his athletes will also be poor attendees or go to a coach who is available. His availability also extends to his being there on race days and also being constantly accessible by telephone for any problems, help or advice. Any coach who feels that he knows all there is to know is misguided. No one should ever stop learning nor fail to realize that there are other methods and ideas which may help and improve his athletes even more. Any coach who is in the sport for his own personal advancement, and not that of his athletes, will never be a successful and fulfilled coach. The successful coach is the one who takes a youngster from being a promising schoolboy through to inter-national honours and major champion ships. The dialogue between coach and pupil will move from being one way in the early days of their partnership to a far more open, two-way dialogue as the athlete matures. During this journey the coach is working towards ultimate redundancy, so that by the time his athlete is competing at a major championship he is no longer the coach but an advisor, confidant and friend.

CHAPTER 2
The Requirements for Success

INTRODUCTION

The successful middle-distance runner requires many qualities, all of which have to be developed if the athlete is to fulfil his potential. These are: speed, strength, stamina (endurance), speed-endurance, strength-endurance, strength at speed (power), suppleness (mobility), style (technique) and psychology. They are interlinked (*see* Fig. 3) and interdependent and have different roles with differing degrees of emphasis in the training programme. To understand each we need to look at it to show what its function is, to demonstrate what type of training will improve the function further and to illustrate the role of each in the race situation.

The importance of each physiological function is shown in the percentage breakdown of the energy systems in the six endurance events (*see* Fig. 4). The table shows how important each of the qualities is to each of the middle-distance events (*see* Fig. 5). The more successful high-performance middle-distance runners develop each of the required qualities to its maximum extent.

In this chapter we look at the main qualities and the additional requirements that are essential for success as a high-performance middle-distance runner. These extra requirements include time management, planning and preparation, nutrition, tactics and a network of support systems. In subsequent chapters we consider the types of training, planning and preparation and in much greater detail.

SPEED

An athlete's muscle fibre determines his basic speed. However, training to maximum speed should not be neglected or ignored. This is a common fault with athletes who lack speed: the tendency is for athletes to work on their stronger qualities and neglect their weaker ones. Pure speed or absolute speed, as it is sometimes referred to, is unlike speed endurance in that it is improved by training over distances of from 50m up to 120m. This type of training primarily uses the alactate or ATP system (*see* Chapter 3). Training by using this system lasts for a maximum of 15sec and enables the athlete to improve both his basic speed and his ability to react quickly in a race. Pure or absolute speed cannot be maintained for the full duration of a middle-distance race, therefore any speed-orientated training is designed to improve the athlete's optimum speed during it. Certainly, training to improve absolute speed, if carried out successfully, will improve an athlete's performance during the middle-distance events.

Speed can be improved by downhill running, sprint drills, acceleration sprints, skills sprinting, up-and-down the clock sessions and dynamic stretching. An up-the-clock session, for example, could be six

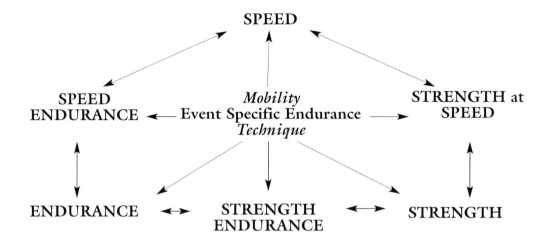

Fig.3. The figure shows the interrelationship of the endurance components – how strength-endurance, speed-endurance and strength at speed (power) are interlinked and dependent on the main components of speed, endurance and strength. It also shows the importance and relationship of these components to technique, mobility and, most importantly, event-specific endurance.

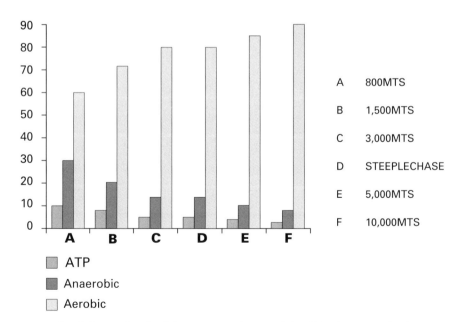

Fig.4. The percentage breakdown of each of the energy pathways of the ATP-CP, anaerobic-lactate and the aerobic system required for each of the endurance events is shown as a block graph. The training programme should be tailored to cater for these percentage breakdowns to meet the specific demands of each event. Therefore an 800m runner would be required to include far more training for the ATP-CP and anaerobic-lactate systems, but far less aerobic training than a marathon runner.

EVENT	800M	1500M	5/10K	S/C	MAR	WLKS
MOBILITY	–	–	–	–	–	–
ENDURANCE (02)	–	–	–	–	–	–
SPEED (ALACTATE)	–	–	–	–		
SPEED ENDURANCE (LA02)	–	–	–	–		
STRENGTH	–	–	–	–		
STRENGTH ENDURANCE	–	–	–	–	–	–
POWER	–	–		–		
TECHNIQUE	–	–	–	–	–	–
TACTICS	–	–	–	–	–	–

OVERVIEW

800m	All aspects
1500m	All aspects but % difference to 800m
5k/10k	No power & little strength and lactate
Steeplechase	All aspects + extra technique
Marathon	Predominantly 02 system
Walks	Predominantly 02 system + emphasis on technique

Fig.5. Using the endurance components (Fig. 3) and the percentages of each event (Fig.4) an overview of the main requirements for each of the endurance events can be obtained. This is shown in diagrammatic form to ensure that the correct requirements for each event are included in the training programme.

repetitions commencing at 30m and progressing in 10m intervals up to 80m, and a down-the-clock session would be the reverse of this. While this training is being carried out, relaxation procedures should also be performed and attention should be paid to the athlete's technique. The recoveries between the repetitions in these activities should be complete, so that maximum speed can be achieved on each repetition.

Training for speed should take place throughout the season. During the preparatory phases it will take the form of drills, up and down the clock sessions and acceleration sprints. These sessions can take place after steady-state running sessions or be incorporated into other training routines. The emphasis should also be on technique and relaxation as well as speed training. As the athlete moves into the pre-competitive and competitive periods, downhill running, sprint skills running and flat-out sprints form not only the more important sessions but also individual specific sessions. Once again, there should be a strong emphasis on technique and relaxation.

The ability to monitor, maintain and increase speed is clearly essential to all middle-distance runners. The athlete must be able to regulate and increase his speed as he approaches the end of a race, during a race to cover any variations in speed and also be able to follow a sustained pace. Moreover, the athlete must have the crucial ability to react instantly to any of these situations.

STRENGTH

Strength implies the use of maximum tension, or the greatest force that is possible with a single muscle contraction. In middle-distance training therefore, the main focus of strength training is on the development of muscular strength. This ensures that a sound strength base is built, developed and maintained; from this all the other qualities can emanate.

It is important that strength training takes place throughout the year. It should not be stopped when the pre-competitive period has been entered otherwise all the strength that has been gained will be lost by the time the competitive climax is reached. The greatest amount of strength work is done during the preparation period. As the pre-competitive and competitive periods are entered, the number of sessions, number of activities and the number of repetitions should decrease.

If weight training is used to build up strength it is preferable to use loads of 85–100 per cent of the athlete's maximum lifting ability, with a low number of repetitions and a high number of sets to get the most beneficial effect. The weight-training exercises used, however, must also be practised the whole year round, be specific to endurance running and be in the ratio of three leg exercises to two abdominal exercises to one arm exercise. It is also important that, if free weights are used, the correct technique is employed and that there are also 'spotters' on either side of the lifter for safety reasons.

Strength in the race situation is not as obvious nor as visible as the other qualities. However, it is one of the core qualities which allows for the development of the other more essential ones. It is particularly important at the climax of a race or in major championships when the athlete has to undertake a number of races to reach the final.

ENDURANCE

Endurance training primarily uses the oxygen transportation system. This means improving the efficiency of the heart, improving the blood circulation to increase the athlete's maximum volume up-take of oxygen and ensuring that there is an efficient exchange and transportation of gases. Its purpose is to produce a more efficient energy production system related to the demands of high-performance middle-distance running. This type of training therefore is *aerobic* and involves a great deal of training. It requires much steady state-running, punctuated by *fartlek* training, long, steady-state runs, alternating the pace runs, extensive interval training and tempo runs. The emphasis is on steady output rather than intensity. The steady-state runs would be over distances of from 4 to 6 miles, while the longer, steady-state runs would of at least an hour's duration.

An accurate measure of aerobic training is the athlete's heart rate. This type of training should normally fall into the region of 120 to 160 beats/min, although it may go higher during certain aspects of alternating pace training, *fartlek* sessions and tempo runs. Endurance training should take place the whole year round, but the main endurance base is built in the preparation period when the greatest mileage is achieved. As the pre-competitive and the competitive period are entered, the number of sessions and the total mileage decreases. The endurance training during this latter period, as well as maintaining the endurance base of the athlete, also helps to get rid of any waste products and stiffness that linger from the high intensity sessions.

Endurance training is the key element in all middle-distance training. Without a good base upon which to draw none of the other qualities, such as speed, speed-endurance or power, can be utilized as effectively in the race situation. The ability to improve an athlete's maximum oxygen uptake ensures that he not only takes in enough to meet the demands of the race but is also able to combat any changes in intensity that are required.

SPEED-ENDURANCE

The intensity of effort involved in speed-endurance training is much higher than that associated with endurance training since the athlete is working to offset the build up of lactic acid. Therefore this type of training is *anaerobic*. The importance of speed-endurance in relation to speed and endurance are illustrated in Fig. 6 on primary energy

ATP-PC & LA SYSTEMS.					ATP-PC, LA & OXYGEN SYSTEMS.				O2 SYSTEM.	
% AEROBIC										
0	10	20	30	40	50	60	70	80	90	100
100	90	80	70	60	50	40	30	20	10	0
% ANAEROBIC										
100	200			400	800	1,500	3,000	5,000	10,000	Mar
10s	20s			45s	1.45s	3.45s	9m	14m	29m	2h15m

Non Shaded Area = Predominance of One Pathway over the Other.

Shaded Area = Events in which both Pathways are of Nearly Equal Importance.

Fig.6. The primary energy systems are show with the aerobic continuum at the top of the page rising from 0 to 100 per cent. As the aerobic percentage rises, the ATP-CP and anaerobic continuum at the foot of the page, which begins at 100 per cent, begins to diminish. The shaded area between 40 and 60 per cent aerobic and 60 and 40 per cent anaerobic is the critical area where both pathways have an important role in the training of middle-distance runners.

pathways. This shows the relationship of the anaerobic and the aerobic requirement for the middle-distance events.

This type of training will include flat-out, 100 per cent effort repetitions at above or below the race distance, high-intensity interval work, quality interval work and repetition work, all over distances of between 100 and 1,000m. In all these sessions the number of repetitions will be low, the recoveries long and involving more than one set, and the intensity of effort will be high. In many cases with this type of training the athlete cannot take in enough oxygen to meet the demands of the training session and cannot therefore stop the build-up of lactic acid. This means that the quality of the training session will deteriorate or will have to be stopped. This inability to take in the required amount of oxygen leaves a deficiency in oxygen uptake and is often referred to as 'oxygen debt'. The athlete's heart rate during speed endurance repetition sessions will be well in excess of 170 beats/min, and in some cases with the high-performance athlete as high as 200.

Although there will be a certain amount of speed-endurance work done throughout the athletic year, the main emphasis with this type of training will be during the pre-competitive and competitive periods. At this time a variety of methods will be used to ensure that, once the competitive climax approaches, the athlete is in the peak of condition.

These types of session are important to ensure that there is an efficient blood supply to the muscles and a high tolerance of both oxygen debt and waste products. The training sessions are also to improve the ability to remove and reuse the waste products that accumulate in the body when working at this level of intensity. In a middle-distance race this is of paramount importance; the longer the athlete can maintain his oxygen intake and offset the build-up of lactic acid, not only will he be stronger at the climax of the race but he will

also become a more efficient and more successful runner.

STRENGTH-ENDURANCE

This is sometimes referred to as local muscular endurance. It is the athlete's ability to continue to use his muscles while fatigue is setting in and he is trying to maintain the quality of his performance. The stronger the muscle, the better its adaptation to the demands of the event. The methods most used for this type of training are circuit training, stage training, long uphill running, repetition work, resistance work against the environment or against a force, the Oregon circuit and back-to-back repetitions. These types of training session are sometimes referred to as 'conditioning work'.

Similar to strength training, strength-endurance training should continue throughout the year. The main emphasis with this type of training will be during the preparation phase. A weekly session as a minimum should be part of the training programme during this period. Once the pre-competition and competition periods are entered the sessions will not only be fewer in number but also frequency.

Strength endurance is a fundamental part of conditioning and a key ingredient in the race situation. This is particularly the case in championship race situations where there are a number of rounds to negotiate. The stronger the athlete, particularly after three or four rounds of competition, the better placed he is to maintain his technique under pressure, offset the build up of lactic acid and utilize his speed to full effect.

POWER

Sometimes called strength at speed or explosive strength. Power is the capacity of athletes to utilize their strength at speed. It is characterized by the ability to react explosively to any given situation. The following methods are those most often employed in the improvement of power: hopping, plyometrics, bounding, weight training, resistance work, weighted belts and short hill work. Depth jumping (*see* Chapter 4) may also be used but only with the mature experienced athlete and only in a safe environment. Power must always be developed alongside technique work.

Elements of power training will take place throughout the year. However, the main focus for power training will be during the pre-competitive and competitive periods when the athlete will become sharper, dynamic and more focused. The more powerful the athlete, the better equipped he will be to react to any given race situation. He is able to react explosively or accelerate dramatically if and when the situation warrants it. Of all the middle-distance events, power is more important in the 800m than in any other.

EVENT-SPECIFIC ENDURANCE

Event-specific endurance is perhaps the key requirement for any middle-distance runner.

It is a mixture of speed (alactate system), speed-endurance (anaerobic-lactate system) and endurance (aerobic system), carefully integrated to meet the specific requirements of the chosen event. The proportions for this mixture for an 800m runner would be: 10 per cent alactate, 30 per cent anaerobic-lactate and 60 per cent aerobic. Event-specific training involves the set number of repetitions totalling the race distance with each one being run at the required race pace.

TECHNIQUE

Technique is clearly of vital importance to the middle-distance runner. Therefore a good basic technical model is required from an early age, any incorrect movements of either the arms or the head are both wasteful and energy consuming. In addition, any incorrect leg movement can be a hindrance in a sprint finish and lead to either under- or over-striding. Moreover, an incorrect foot plant can lead to pronation and injury.

The ideal technique (*see* Fig. 7 and 8) is relaxed, economical and efficient. To aid technique development, the coach's eye, video analysis and digital sequential analysis

Fig.7. The whole running sequence is depicted in this technical model showing the support, flight and return to the support phase. The foot position at touchdown varies with the running pace. The leg swings forward with an open knee, with the lower leg nearly parallel to the ground. The thigh in the forward position at the maximum extension of the drive allows the hip, leg and foot to complete the movement. The free leg is then at its greatest flexion and is able to swing through to replace the front leg. The knee lift is lower and the arm movement is less pronounced than for a sprinter (except when the middle-distance runner is involved in a sprint finish). The head is held erect and, along with the shoulders, neck and arms, should be relaxed. The trunk should be relaxed and erect at all times. The arms swing gently forward and slightly across the chest at an angle of approximately 90 degrees.

Fig.8. The phase structure of the running technical model may be broken down into rear support phase, rear swinging phase, front swinging phase and front support phase. The rear support phase function is the production of force for the forward drive and the upward swing of the thigh of the leading leg. The foot, being planted straight ahead, achieves this, allowing an extension in the foot, knee and hip. The trunk should be upright but leaning slightly forward, with the head upright and the shoulders and facial muscles relaxed. The elbow angle should be at 90 degrees, with arms swinging forward and then backwards and upwards. The hands are relaxed and held as an open fist. The rear swinging phase function makes preparation for the knee lift and allows for relaxation. The rear leg is relaxed and swings backwards and upwards with an inactive heel lift to the buttock. This is the start of the rapid and active forward swing of the thigh to produce the forward stride. The front swinging phase function is to bring the foot forward in preparation for landing and to determine the length of stride. The thigh swings forward and upward with the height of the knee being determined by the running speed. The backward lowering of the thigh initiates landing into the front support phase, the arms providing balance and support. The front support phase function is to absorb the weight of the body on landing and prepare for the rapid drive into the next running stride. The foot is placed on the ground on the outer edge of the ball of the foot, in approximately the vertical position to allow for the absorption of the runner's body weight. The knee will give only slightly so that the point of ground contact is not too far in front of the body's centre to ensure there is no braking effect.

can be used. In this way each separate segment of the technique – head, trunk, arms and legs – can be analysed in both isolation and in relation to the whole movement. By using these methods of feedback, athletes can see any problems with their technique and rectify them during training sessions.

The technique of a high-performance middle-distance runner has a good ratio of stride length to stride frequency, which he adjusts according to the pace requirements of the race. The head is more upright than in sprinting. However, as with the sprinter, the shoulders should remain still and the arms move in the direction of the race. Too great or too active a torque across the front of the body is to be avoided. The elbows should remain beside the body. The high-performance middle-distance runner's foot, unlike the sprinter's, lands first on the outer edge of the middle of the foot. The foot then tips inward on to the whole sole and when under the weight of the whole body the heel touches the ground.

In the athlete's early years and during the transition phase, work should be done on technique so that it does not disintegrate under pressure. It is also advisable to include technique work in training sessions if the athlete is returning after injury. This will then stop any overcompensating by the athlete, who may be sub-consciously protecting his previous injury. Technique can be improved by sprint drills, dynamic stretching and core stability and during training sessions. Practice is permanent, correct practice is perfection.

The ability of an athlete to be as economical and as effective as possible during the race is of paramount importance. This ensures that he approaches the end of the race in the best possible condition. At this stage, he should be able to maintain his technique and keep relaxed, while others are tensing up and losing form as the effects of the race and lactic acid take their toll.

MOBILITY

A full range of movement is essential to the middle-distance runner if he is to use his physiological assets to the full. Mobility and suppleness begin to wane from the age of eight onwards and therefore it is crucial that

flexing and stretching exercises are part of the training programme. The muscles that cause the movement to take place in any joint action are called the protagonists. Opposing this movement and determining the mobility of the joint are the muscles and tissues being stretched. These are the antagonists. In any movement these two groups of muscles work in harmony, one set causing the action and the other opposing it.

Fig.9. This is a good exercise for stretching the quadriceps muscles. This group of muscles tends to get neglected in mobility exercises. The foot is pulled towards the buttock and held for a period and the action is then repeated with the other leg. Care is needed with both balance and the strain on the knee joint. Photo: Spencer G. Duval

Fig.10. Sitting with the legs wide apart, walk the hands as far forwards as possible without lifting the knees and hold. Then move the hands to left and right to the outside of each leg, keeping the chest as low as possible. Repeat three times to each side. This is a good exercise for the lower back, groin, abdominals and hamstrings.

Fig.11. Sitting as in the figure with the soles of the feet together in front, elbows then move out so that they are on the inside of each knee. Gently press the knees outwards and downwards for six repetitions. This exercise helps with hip rotation and the stretching of the groin area (adductors and abductors).

Fig.12. Sit in the hurdle position on the ground with the sole of the trail leg placed against the lead leg. Move the hands as far down the lead leg as possible until it is painful. Then stretch a little further and repeat on both legs. This is another good exercise for the hips, lower back and hamstrings.

Fig.14. Another exercise to stretch the quadriceps muscles. Lie flat on the ground and lift the leg as shown in the picture, with a bent knee. Hold the knee area and pull backward and downward to feel the stretch. Repeat on both legs. Photo: Spencer G. Duval

Fig.13. An exercise to stretch the hamstring muscles. One leg is crossed over in front of the other, keeping the rear leg straight. Slowly, but with no bouncing effect, stretch as far as possible with the hands down the front leg and then stretch further. Hold each repetition for 10sec and then repeat on the other leg. This exercise is specific to each leg. Photo: Spencer G. Duval

Fig.15. Both athletes are stretching the groin areas (adductors and abductors). The weight is taken on the leg that is square to the floor and the extended leg is gently pushed downwards, either with the hand (as shown in the foreground) or without the hands (as shown at rear of the figure). The legs are then changed and the exercise repeated.

In mobility training the aim is to improve the range of movement by stretching the antagonist muscles slightly further.

The optimum time for mobility and flexibility is when the body is warm. Therefore it is advisable to do the exercises later in the day and not first thing in the morning. The mobility exercises should preferably be done daily, throughout the year as well as any mobility work done in a warm-up session. A full range of exercises may be undertaken and they may be active, passive or kinetic exercises, or can be incorporated into a dynamic stretching routine

Active mobility exercises involve a slow stretch as far as it is possible for the athlete to reach. The position is then held for 10 to 12sec. The stretch position is then released, relaxed and the exercise repeated. Passive mobility exercises are performed with either a partner or a piece of equipment to provide the force that stretches the muscles. With the more experienced athlete the partner can

Fig.16. Although an arm exercise, this also helps to open up the muscles at the front of the chest as well as helping the back. Pull the arm back over the head and then gently push it down the back. Repeat with both arms, holding for 10sec each. Photo: Spencer G. Duval

Fig.18. This exercise to stretch the calf muscles can be done against any solid, upright object. Keep the feet shoulder-width apart and the rear leg straight. Lean the hips towards the object. The exercise should be held for 10sec and then the legs alternated. Photo: Spencer G. Duval

Fig.17. In the sitting position shown in the picture, the right elbow pushes against the left knee. This is a good exercise for the hip-flexor area and also for the hamstring of the lead leg, which must be kept straight. Hold for 10sec and then repeat on the other leg.

Fig.19. For this hamstring stretch choose a raised object as shown in the picture which should be at the appropriate height. Put the heel of one leg on it, straighten the leg and slowly lean forward towards the foot. Keep the leg straight and bring the head and chest down to the leg. Hold the final position and then repeat with the other leg. The support leg must remain static and straight to act as a support. Photo: Spencer G. Duval

Fig.20. Improvisation is sometimes the answer. In this picture the athlete is using her partner before the race as a static object so that she can stretch her calf muscles.Photo: Spencer G. Duval

assist by using the PNF method (proprioceptive neuromuscular facilitation) and the '3PIC' method (stretch contract, contract and stretch). With the PNF method the partner forces the muscle until the athlete feels discomfort, the muscle is then held for 6 to 10sec, relaxed and repeated three to four times. This is an isometric exercise that contracts the antagonist muscles (*see* Fig. 21 to 24). The PNF exercises immediately followed by the 3PIC

Fig.21. (above right) In this exercise the athlete is unable to get her two hands to meet. This exercise, if done correctly, will not only stretch her arms but also the pectoral muscles and help to straighten the back.

Fig.22. (right) Using the PNF method, her partner gently assists her so that the exercise can be completed and holds the arms in the required position for the time of the exercise. The arms are then changed over. Most athletes will naturally find that they are more flexible with one of their arms than with the other.

Fig.23. Lying on the back with arms outstretched and feet together in a crucifix position. Take the opposite leg, keeping it straight, across the body to try and touch the opposite hand. This is good for stretching the hip flexors, hamstring and gluteus muscles as well as for hip rotation.

Fig.24. With this PNF exercise the athlete is gently assisted by a partner to achieve the position required in Fig.23. The leg is held at its furthest position for a set period and then the legs are changed over.

Fig.25. (right) The aim of all the hurdle drills is to improve coordination, mobility and stability. In this exercise the athlete is using the inside leg to come over on the outside of the hurdle. The body has to remain upright, eyes ahead and the outside leg stable. This is a good exercise for the hip flexor, gluteus, abductor and adductor muscles.

set of exercises produce an active contraction of the protagonist muscles. The exercise is held for 3 to 6sec, relaxed and repeated three to four times. Kinetic mobility exercises involving swinging or rotating the limbs backwards and forwards through their range of movement may also be used.

Mobility exercises may also involve coordination techniques. Using six to eight hurdles placed together in a row (*see* Fig. 25 and 26) the athlete has to walk down the side of the hurdles with the inside trail leg going over the outside of the hurdles. The second exercise involves stepping over the middle of the hurdles by using the same leg at each hurdle. Once this has been completed the exercise is repeated with the other leg (*see* Fig. 27 and 28). The second exercise involves alternate legs leading over the hurdles in the same sequence. In this exercise, once the leading leg has touched the ground at the other side of the hurdle, the trailing leg follows through over the next hurdle to land on the floor. This is repeated with alternate legs all the way down the hurdles (*see* Fig. 29 and 30). As well as being

Fig.26. This is the conclusion of the hurdle drill in Fig.25. Here the trail leg has come through into the running phase with the hips remaining high. The exercise should then be repeated, leading with the other leg. Another drill is side skipping with a bent leg over the middle of the row of hurdles, repeating with the other leg leading. This exercise stretches and strengthens the hamstring and gluteus muscles. It may be done with either a slow or a fast trail leg action. The same exercise may then be done over the middle of the hurdles.

Fig.27. With this exercise the athletes are stepping over the row of hurdles using the same leg at each. Then, after two or three repetitions, they will repeat the exercise, leading with the other leg. The athlete needs to be stable, hips held high and on the balls of his feet during this exercise.

Fig.28. This is a side view of the exercise in Fig.27, showing the leg coming through to be placed on the ground. This particular exercise is for stretching the gluteus and hamstring muscles and helping with hip rotation. With a tall athlete, the hurdles for the exercise may be raised and placed further apart.

an excellent mobility exercise for the hip and pelvic area, the exercises also strengthen this area, develop coordination skills and improve the range of movement.

The more flexible and supple the athlete, the greater his range of movement. This means that in any race he will be more economical and cover more ground efficiently. If an athlete, for example, is losing a centimetre on every stride because poor flexibility is restricting his range of movement, he could lose up to 12m during

Fig.29. In this exercise the athletes have to move down the row of hurdles, which are close together, using alternate legs at each. This means that they have to reach out and extend their lead leg. The athletes have to remain tall and have high knees. This exercise is for hip mobility and really stretches the hip flexors.

Fig.30. This side shot of the same exercise as Fig.29 shows the athlete's lead leg passing over the hurdle from where it will stretch out to get as near to the hurdle as possible. This is to help the trail leg when it comes through to go over the hurdle. Another exercise that can be used with the row of hurdles is side skipping: going over the side of the hurdles with a bounce, the leg is kept straight and this is then repeated with the other leg on the other side. This exercise stretches both the hamstring and the hip flexor. All these drills may be used as hurdle endurance sessions, where the athlete has to concentrate on all the above points while the body is in a fatigued state. As well as improving coordination, hurdle drills also improve an athlete's range of movement and strengthen his tendon-ligament system to help to prevent injury.

an 800m race, and obviously more the further he runs. Naturally, this will have a profound effect on an athlete's performance in the race. Mobility will also aid his technique in the race and help him to react smoothly and efficiently to any explosive reaction that may be required. It also helps the athlete to steer clear of injury, and, if he does succumb to it, it enables him to recover more quickly than the athlete who is less flexible.

SUPPORT SYSTEMS

The function of any support system is to help to facilitate the athlete's needs. This then ensures that he is as prepared as he can be for his competition. To ensure that every eventuality is covered, a number of support systems have to be put in place. By building up a network of support systems, the high-performance athlete becomes proactive rather than reactive to any situation or development that may occur. The support systems are not essential for the athlete's success as a high-performance athlete, but they are highly desirable support aids that allow training and racing to take place without any problems (*see* Fig. 31). Such a network could mark the difference between an athlete becoming a successful high-performance middle-distance runner or one just aspiring to be so. One could also define

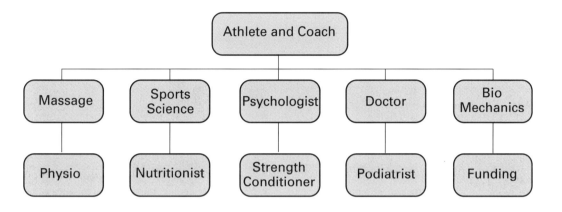

Fig.31. Support systems: the different types are shown and the value of each is set out in Chapters 2 and 5.

the difference between being seriously injured or being able to diagnose a problem quickly and prevent it from being exacerbated.

The following should be included in an ideal support network system: physiotherapist, nutritionist, masseur, psychologist, physiologist, biomechanics specialist, doctor, podiatrist and financial facilitator/adviser. The most important objective of the support network is to maximize rest and regeneration for the athlete. Indeed, the central concept of the support system is that it is athlete-centred. This ensures that the athlete enters the race healthy, fit, injury-free and in the best possible shape, both physically and mentally. Then there can be no excuses for a poor performance.

TACTICS

To ensure that all the hard work that has gone into the training programme reaches fruition, it is imperative that the athlete goes into a race with prearranged race tactics, and that these are successfully implemented. A variety of methods can be included and adopted in training to simulate both tactical

awareness and the execution of the tactics (*see* Chapter 7). These methods include the use of short sprints, long sprints, intermittent pace repetitions, increasing the pace repetitions, leading the pace throughout, acceleration sprints, reaction drills and an increased pace in the middle of the repetitions. These training methods are to facilitate the tactics in the race and may be practised throughout the year. The devised tactics will comprise one of the above or a combination of them. They must be executed at the correct time, at the correct spot and with the athlete's being in the correct place to fulfil them. However, the plan should be flexible enough so that the athlete can adapt if anything or everything goes wrong.

PSYCHOLOGICAL

Psychological preparation is necessary to ensure that the athlete is perfectly calm and relaxed, and also confident, without being overconfident before the start of a race. He must also be in control of his emotions since these could affect his performance. He should also be totally committed to, and be concentrating exclusively on, the forthcoming race. The coach must ensure that his athlete is prepared both physically and mentally, and this is achieved during the training sessions. It is the coach's role to know his athlete and to energize and motivate him as required. This is achieved only after a great deal of interaction between coach and athlete. The coach must appear calm at all times, since nervous coaches make nervous athletes. It is the role of the coach to give the athlete confidence, particularly in the way he is performing in training, so that the athlete can take this confidence and transfer it to the race.

Many races are lost before the athlete even steps on to the track or because the athlete loses confidence during the race. He has to be strong mentally as well as physically and have confidence in his own ability. He also has to have confidence in how his training has progressed and in his chosen tactical plan. Otherwise all the hard work that has gone before will not be put to the maximal use.

Fig.32. This shows a high-performance athlete about to undertake a steady run. Because she has a young child she maximizes her time-management skills and uses a purpose-built buggy, which has been adapted so that she can do her training and take her young child with her on the run. In this way she not only gets her steady run done while still supervising the child but also frees up time for another training session later in the day.

TIME MANAGEMENT

Time management is crucially important, particularly to the high-performance athlete since he has so much to fit into his hectic schedule. It also appropriate to the talented junior athlete who moves away from home for the first time either to go to a university or college or find employment. Similarly, a female international athlete who has recently become a mother has to look for ways to fit in the training sessions around coping with the addition to the family (see Fig. 32). She has to adapt to a completely new routine and cope with being self-sufficient. Without proper time management, planning and preparation, all the rest of the hard work, support and training can flounder. Time management can only facilitate the specifics of any training programme. It is like the network of support systems, that is, not a required element for a high-performance middle-distance runner, but, if correctly implemented, it allows all the other elements to be fully developed in the training sessions. It also allows the runner time for rest and regeneration, a key component of the training programme. Time management is of great importance on race days, and particularly at major championships, when the athlete is likely to be living in a competitors' village and have his races spread over a number of days. The idea is to ensure that the athlete is correctly prepared and as fresh and rested as possible for the key race of the season.

NUTRITION

An athlete's body is like a Rolls-Royce car and therefore deserves to have the best fuel available put into it. This means having the correct carbohydrate loading, proteins, vitamins, minerals, fats and fibre in the diet.

Carbohydrates are the main source of energy; bread, sugars, pasta, potatoes, rice and cakes are among the most common carbohydrate foods. Proteins are essential to growth and the repair of muscle and other body tissues; they can be found in such foods as vegetables, dairy products, meat, chicken, fish, milk and nuts. Vitamins play an important role in many of the body's chemical processes; different vitamins can be found in a variety of foodstuffs but be supplemented by multivitamin pills. It is of particular importance to take supplements for vitamin B (essential for energy production) and vitamin C (linked to oxygen transport and energy production). Both of these are water-soluble and therefore, because of the processes of cooking and storage, you cannot assume that the products that contain them will have the required amounts when they are eaten. The body's stores become depleted during strenuous training and during competition and therefore they need to be replenished.

Minerals are critical to the normal functioning of the body. Most diets contain sufficient quantities of them to meet the body's needs, nonetheless, because of the excessive demands of training and perspiration, it is advisable for the athlete to take supplements in either tablet or liquid form. Fats are a source of energy and are important in relation to vitamins. However, because of the length of time fatty foods take to digest and the fact that it takes more oxygen to release energy from fats than from carbohydrates, it is best to limit the intake of fats. Fibre intake is important for the health of the digestive system; wholemeal bread and bran flakes are two examples of foods that supply the essential roughage. It is critical that the athlete, particularly after an intense training session, does not eat junk food or snacks. The food that he takes on board at this time should be appropriate to his requirements, help him repair bodily tissue and ensure that he keeps fit and healthy.

Racing is similar to training in that the body needs nourishing and invigorating and it is of particular importance that plenty of fluids are taken on board to help hydration. The fluid intake is crucial at all times and particularly in hot weather and if leading up to a major championship, where there should be a constant intake of fluids and electrolyte drinks both before and during the games. The type of drink used should contain the same salt–water balance as in the body and should be easily absorbed. The drink should also contain vitamin C, which is also lost through perspiration, and should never be ice cold nor have ice in it. It is also better for the athlete to sip the drinks before, during and after competition to replace water and salts lost from the body through perspiration. In a hot, humid climate the body needs to more than double the normal fluid intake. Thirst is not a reliable guide to dehydration – but if you are thirsty you are certainly dehydrated. A strict check should be kept on the bodyweight and the colour of the athlete's urine to ensure that he is not becoming dehydrated.

The qualities of speed, strength, endurance, speed-endurance, strength at speed, power, technique, mobility and mental strength are interlinked, as we have noted (*see* Fig. 3), and must be progressed precisely, at the appropriate time of the year and in the correct proportions and to the correct degree. When applied to the training programme these qualities must be tailored to the individual athlete. The other important requirements – time management, planning and preparation, nutrition, tactics and the support systems – must all be in place to ensure that the training programme of the high-performance middle-distance runner progresses smoothly throughout the year.

CHAPTER 3

Training Methods and Effects

PHYSIOLOGICAL REQUIREMENTS

To understand what effect different types of training and training load have on an athlete an understanding of how the body works is essential. This comprises how the body functions at rest and how its functions change when the body is working at maximum intensity. A knowledge of which processes limit performance and how these limitations can be reduced through training is also necessary. However, all athletes are individuals and will therefore respond differently to the different types of training. Therefore by using the scientific knowledge available the training must be structured to meet each athlete's individual requirements.

Functions and Systems

The body is made up of many inter-dependent and interconnecting parts, of which the most important are the following. The smallest unit or building block in the body is the *cell*, whose processes are controlled by the nucleus, which can adapt to what is required of it, and because of this adaptation training can change the fitness levels.

The body comprises nine systems which work either individually or in conjunction with each other and collectively help the body to function. The *skeletal system* involves movement, protection, support, and calcium storage and blood cell production. The *muscular system* both supports and activates movement. There are three distinct types of muscle tissue found in our bodies: skeletal muscle is attached to bones and is the voluntary, contractile tissue, which moves the skeleton about; knowledge of the structure, function and response to training of this type of muscle is important. Smooth muscle is involuntary muscle and is found in the walls of the tubular organs such as the digestive, circulatory and respiratory systems; these muscles are concerned with the movement through these systems and their action is spontaneous. Cardiac muscle is an involuntary muscle found only in the heart, it contracts on its own, constantly and without becoming fatigued. Muscle fibres fall into two categories: red or slow twitch fibres (Type I), characterised by a greater endurance capacity but a relative slow action and using predominantly aerobic sources; and the opposite white or fast twitch muscle fibres (Type II), characterized by a high speed of contraction but relatively low endurance capabilities and using predominantly anaerobic and glycolytic pathways. Because these two types of muscle fibre are the extreme opposites of each other, intermediary types of fibre have now been identified (*see* Fig. 33).

The fast twitch fibres group (Type II) may be sub-divided into an intermediary group, between the slow and the fast twitch fibres, known as Type IIa. The pure fast twitch fibre is known as Type IIb. The intermediary Type IIa shares features of both

Table of Muscle Fibres

	Type I slow twitch (st) oxidative	Type IIa fast twitch (fta) oxidative glycolytic	Type IIb fast twitch (ftb) glycolytic
aerobic or oxidative capacity	high	moderately high	low
anaerobic or glycolytic capacity	low	high	highest
number of mitochondria	high	intermediate	low
contractile speed	slow	fast	fastest
fatigue resistance	high	moderate	low

Fig.33. Diagram showing the classification and characteristics of the several muscle-fibre types.

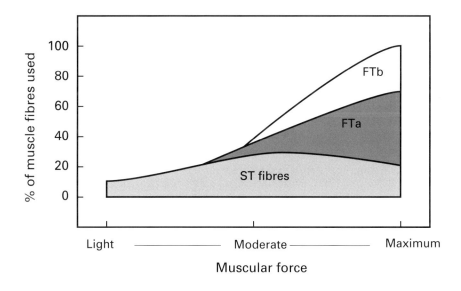

Fig.33a. A cross-section of the different muscle fibres showing the relationship between intensity and the utilization of fast and slow twitch fibres during exercise. (After R. Uebel, 1987)

muscle Types I and IIb and may be thought of as fast twitch, oxidative-glycolytic fibres. This fibre is able to obtain the energy it requires from both the oxidative pathways or the anaerobic glycolytic pathways. (Fig. 33a is a cross-section of the muscle fibres.)

All of these movements and actions are planned, initiated and coordinated by the *nervous system*. The motor unit is the fundamental unit for muscle contraction and innervates muscle fibres of a single type. The integrated processes of recruitment, summation and synchronization achieve muscle control and regulation. Specific neuro-muscular training will contribute to a more efficient system. The *circulatory system* ensures that the heart sends the oxygenated blood around the body efficiently. It carries oxygen from the lungs to the body cells, as well as nutrients and hormones to them. It also takes carbon dioxide and other waste products away from the cells and heat to the skin's surface to maintain a constant internal body temperature. It is a system that adapts well to training. Understanding how the system responds and so adapts and its role in oxygen transportation is essential when designing a training programme.

The *respiratory system* is responsible for providing the body with oxygen and bringing it into close contact with the blood and for the exchange of gases with the environment. It is important to note the level of environmental pollution and the risk of asthma. Improvement in an individual's VO2 maximum is a reflection of an improvement of the function of the cardio-respiratory system and the total capacity for aerobic work. The *immune system* provides a line of resistance and defence against invading bacteria, parasites and viruses. It depends on the actions of specialized cells and antibodies, which eliminate or neutralize these invaders which may cause illness. Unfortunately, one of the most serious consequences of heavy training is the negative effect it has on the body's immune system. Short bouts of intense exercise can temporarily impair the immune response and successive days of heavy training can amplify this suppression, increasing an athlete's susceptibility to infections. Furthermore, intense exercise during illness might decrease the ability to fight off infection and increase the risk of even greater complications.

The *digestive system* breaks down food and prepares it for absorption into the blood system. The *excretory system* deals with the elimination of the waste products from the body. The final system the *endocrine* or *hormonal system* is involved with the production of chemical messages that regulate the body's functions.

The systems can also work together, for example, the skeletal and the muscular systems function together and are referred to as the *musculo-skeletal system*. Skilled movement is the result of the coordinated activity of the nervous and the muscular system, referred to collectively as the *neuro-muscular system*. Any drill which assists the athlete in the development of his coordination can be referred to as a neuro-muscular exercise. The circulatory and the respiratory system cooperate in transporting oxygen to where it is needed and form the *cardio-respiratory system*.

Homeostasis describes the maintenance of a stable environment within the body, which is essential for it to operate effectively. It is achieved through the combined actions of the nervous and the endocrine systems. The provision for this stable environment, even when external conditions and pressures are making their demands felt, is a whole body function. It involves compensatory mechanisms which influence the cells to act as a whole and adapt to these changes, including the demands of training. Conditions which require control through homeostasis are: body temperature, blood pressure, blood glucose levels, fluid and water balance, and the oxygen and carbon dioxide concentrations in the blood. The hormones are the guardians of homeostasis, they regulate organic functions through their individual and combined roles. An understanding of hormone function is essential in determining an athlete's fitness level, his health and the impact on his recovery. Using this knowledge the coach and his athlete have to ensure that the training regime has the correct effect.

Distance (m)	ATP-CP (%)	Anaerobic-Lactate (%)	Aerobic (%)
100	25	70	5
200	15	60	25
400	12	43	45
800	10	30	60
1,500	8	20	72
3,000	5	15	80
5,000	4	10	86
10,000	3–2	12–8	85–90
Marathon	0	5–2	95–98

Fig. 34. Shares of energy supply mechanisms during middle-distance track events (according to Mader).

A middle-distance runner has to tailor his training to the physiological demands of his event. The three predominant energy pathways he uses are: the *alactate system*, sometimes referred to as the *ATP-CP system*, the *anaerobic system*, sometimes referred to as the *lactic system*, and the *aerobic system*, sometimes referred to as the *O2 system*. These three systems are interrelated but contribute to differing degrees in the several middle-distance events (Fig. 34). These systems are dependent on both the intensity and the duration of the exercise, all serve as pathways to provide the energy for the re-synthesis of ATP.

None of these three systems can operate efficiently or be trained effectively without the other highly complex systems of the body functioning correctly.

Living cells, with the agency of *adenosine triphosphate (ATP)*, are able to transform the chemical energy potentially available in food into other forms of energy to maintain the normal functions of the body, such as mechanical energy, thermal energy for body heat and electrical energy to conduct nerve impulses. These processes constitute *metabolism*. Exercise will affect the basal metabolic rate of an athlete, which is measured at rest. Metabolism is a remarkable process for providing the energy needed to power the body.

The *alactate system* or *ATP-CP* system functions as follows: ATP is broken down to adenosine diphosphate (ADP) to provide cells with energy for exercise and muscle contraction. The amount of ATP in cells, including muscle cells, is limited and quickly depleted. However, ADP can be re-synthesized back to ATP by the addition of another phosphate group. The two processes – one by which energy is used and the other, producing energy, must be kept in balance, otherwise there could be a lowering of ATP levels. At maximal levels of effort muscle ATP will last for only 1–2sec of activity. ATP-CP (*CP: creatine phosphate*) is activated as the main energy source to provide ATP, but at maximal effort will only provide it for 5–7sec. Therefore by using the ATP in the muscle, plus the re-synthesised ATP produced by the ATP-CP system, maximal exercise can be sustained for 6–9sec; therefore this system will be used predominantly in events such as the 100m.

The *lactate system* will also make a contribution during these short, maximum efforts of exercise. This system becomes the predominant supplier of ATP for longer, controlled, maximum efforts of up to 45sec duration. The lactate system is dependent on glycogen and glucose as fuel for the muscle and involves the process of glycosis, but in this case anaerobic glycosis. Anaerobic glycosis may work in the presence of oxygen but does not require it. It also produces a small amount of ATP quickly and lactic acid. The lactate system is working all the time and not just when the body runs out of oxygen. Lactate is therefore being produced when in the body at rest as well as during exercise.

This system can be sustained for up to 2min of intense exercise, but now the *aerobic system* (involving oxygen) begins to have a gradually increasing contribution. After 2min, the lactic system will no longer be the predominant energy source and the aerobic system will then become the preferred energy source. This system is capable of fuelling relatively low-intensity exercise for a considerable period. The aerobic system is complex and uses carbohydrate, fats and sometimes proteins in the provision of energy. Each of these fuels can eventually be consumed in the presence of oxygen to release energy to re-synthesize ATP.

With this physiological knowledge the training programme devised should ensure that the correct energy pathways relevant to the athlete's event are catered for in the correct proportions and developed at the correct rates. The following are the types of training session which should be used when developing each of the energy pathways. The development of them is known as *total endurance* and is shown in Fig. 35.

To ensure that the correct levels of intensity are adhered to when undertaking the training sessions, the use of a heart-rate monitor can be of value. It has a number of functions, assuming that the athlete is fit and healthy; first, it is a check to ensure that the required heart rates indicated in the training sessions are met. This allows the session to be correctly controlled. If the heart rate is too high, the level of intensity has been set too high for him to reach at this point in the training year. Secondly, it checks that the recovery time is correct. The more rapid the drop in the pulse rate after a repetition, the better the training condition of the athlete. However, if the rate does not drop quickly enough in the time allowed between repetitions it means that the prescribed recovery is insufficient. Thirdly, the heart rate for the aerobic–anaerobic threshold is

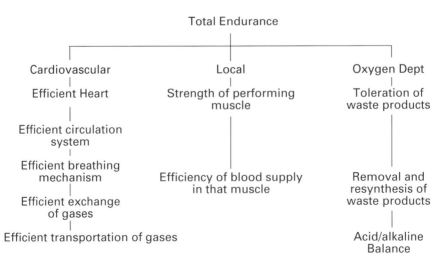

Fig.35: Total endurance has three overlapping aspects: cardiovascular and respiratory endurance (aerobic efficiency), local muscular endurance (strength-endurance) and speed-endurance (anaerobic efficiency). The training effects on each of these are shown here in more detail.

approximately 168 beats/min, therefore, training just below and above this level involves both the aerobic and predominantly the anaerobic energy pathway. Fourthly, the resting pulse rate, which should be taken first thing in the morning, is a good indicator of the athlete's state of health; an unusual increase in the resting pulse rate often indicates the presence of a virus or other infection. Fifthly, the optimum training level or threshold can be deduced by subtracting the resting pulse rate from the rate achieved after the greatest maximum effort. The difference is known as the maximum pulse increase and should be used as a guide when setting the levels for the training programme. An example of this would be:

maximum pulse rate	225
resting pulse rate	35
∴ maximum pulse increase	190

Although not as scientifically accurate as lactate or laboratory testing, heart rate monitors are a useful guide to ensure that the levels of intensity and recoveries are being correctly followed.

TRAINING METHODS

Aerobic System

To understand the responses and adaptations to exercise and training of the cardio-respiratory system and its role in oxygen transport is essential when devising a training programme to improve aerobic capacity. The main duration methods involving the oxygen transportation system are:
• continuous long distance running
• continuous steady state running
• recovery run
• fast aerobic run or tempo run
• alternating pace runs

• *fartlek*
• repetition methods

Before any training programme is undertaken the athlete should have an aerobic fitness test to ascertain his level of fitness. The test should be over 45min or 1hr, run at maximum speed, on a flat course. From the distance covered during this run, the speed per kilometre can be calculated. By using this as the basis, the aerobic training methods can then be developed and the proportions at which they need to be run for maximum effect determined. To ensure that the aerobic training is progressing correctly, the runner should be tested again over the same duration and course every four to five weeks. The test will determine the following percentages for the main training methods:

Type	Percentage of test fitness level speed
repetitions	100
tempo run/fast aerobic runs	95
long-distance runs	90
steady-state aerobic runs	85
recovery runs	70

A large proportion of aerobic training will be with heart rates in the range of 120–160 beats/min. It is particularly essential in the preparation phase that a good aerobic base is developed and built up so that the training methods that are used later will yield the maximum benefit. Other tests to predict the maximum oxygen uptake are the Balke test and the multistage fitness test. The first involves running on a track at maximum speed for 15min. The distance covered is referred to a chart which predicts maximum VO2 to an accuracy of 95 per cent. The multistage fitness training involves a series of 20m shuttle runs at increasingly faster speeds, keeping in time to pre-recorded signals until the athlete cannot keep pace with the recording. The shuttle

Fig.36. The long aerobic run should be done at 90 per cent of the athlete's current fitness level, with pulse rates in the 140–165 range. The distance will vary for each athlete, but the aim should be to run for a minimum of 1hr. If possible, it is better to do this sort of training run in daytime and off-road to make it easier on the legs and to add variety to the training programme. Photo: Spencer G. Duval

runs are structured into a series of progressive levels and the highest level achieved is referred to a table, which predicts the VO2 maximum.

The following types of aerobic training, if correctly deployed, will not only build up the aerobic base but the maximum VO2 or aerobic capacity as well. Certain types of aerobic running, such as steady-state runs, recovery runs and long-distance runs, can be done in a group with other athletes. However, to get the maximum benefit, the members of the group must be of a similar ability. Because of the specificity of *fartleks*, alternately paced runs, tempo runs and repetition sessions, it is better to do these individually or in a structured, controlled, small group.

Continuous, long, steady running will be over periods ranging from 45min to well over 1hr. Therefore it is advisable to do this run in daylight away from the traffic in a stress-free environment (*see* Fig. 36). The speed determined by the base fitness test will be at 90 per cent of his maximum, with heart rates in the 140–165 beats/min. Because of the duration of the training run and the speed this is a medium- to high-intensity training session. The following diagram shows how the three energy systems are utilized in an hour's training run at this level of intensity (Fig. 37).

%

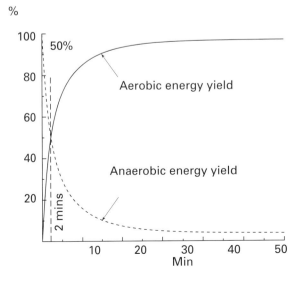

Fig.37. The figure shows the percentage of total energy yield from the aerobic and the anaerobic pathway during maximal efforts up to 1hr in duration for a high-performance middle-distance runner (after Astrand).

Fig.38. Steady-state running is the staple diet of middle-distance training, particularly in the preparatory phases. These training runs should be at 85 per cent of the athlete's current fitness level, with pulse rates in the 120–160 range. Photo: Spencer G. Duval

Fig.39. Recovery runs should always follow a high-intensity training session to help the body get rid of any waste products and to rebuild and re-synthesize body tissues. The recovery run should be done at 70 per cent of the athlete's current fitness level with pulse rates in the 110–130 range. The optimum recovery run would be for 30min and preferably off-road since the legs could be sore and tight from the previous high-intensity session. Photo: Spencer G. Duval

A *steady-state run* is the staple diet of aerobic training. It will be over distances of 10 to 15km, with a heart rate of 120–160 beats/min. The speed of the training run will be at 85 per cent of the fitness test speed. This is a medium-intensity session and is important in both building up the aerobic base and in developing the maximum VO2. Because throughout the year this is a most repeated training unit it helps to vary both the surface and the training environment where possible (*see* Fig. 38).

A *recovery run* is an essential part of aerobic running. It is of low intensity and is run at 70 per cent of the fitness level. The heart rate will be low, with rates in the 110–130 beats/min range. This session should always follow one of high intensity, such as a tempo run or repetition session, to help the body recover and adapt to this type of session. The distance covered in a recovery session should be that taking no more than 30min of running time. If possible, it should be done on a surface which will not impact too much on already fatigued legs (*see* Fig. 39).

The *fast aerobic run*, sometimes incorrectly referred to as a tempo run, is used once per week, if there are no race commitments. This type of training is done at 95 per cent of the fitness level with heart rates of 160–175 beats/min. This type of training is used to replicate the demands required in race running and will also involve, because of its intensity, an anaerobic effect. This is a high-intensity session and should be followed by a low-intensity recovery run. The distances covered in this type of session will vary from between 10 and 12km.

To ensure that not all the training is done at a similar pace, sessions such as an *alternate pace run* may be introduced. This type will be used during a long duration run

Fig.40. A *fartlek* training session involves all the energy pathways, therefore during the session, which should be upwards of 1hr, all the percentage levels of training will be used. Similarly the pulse rates involved will fluctuate between 100 and 180+ beats/min. This type of training session is better suited to a natural environment, if this is feasible. Photo: Spencer G. Duval

with the pace alternating every half-mile or kilometre, from steady to hard and so forth. This type of training will have heart rates fluctuating from 120 beats/min on the steady part to 170+ during the harder bursts. This means that there will be some anaerobic work involved on the faster sections, and the steady sections will help the recovery. This type of training is very beneficial in developing maximum VO2. The steady sections of the training run will be at 85 per cent of his fitness level, whereas the faster sections will be at nearer 95 per cent.

Another, similar session to the alternate paced run session is the *fartlek*, which involves all the energy pathways with short sprints, easy running, hill work, long sustained bursts and steady-state running all mixed together. The duration of the session will be anything from 45min to well over an hour. It will usually be run in a forest, on a golf course, playing fields or parkland. The demands of the environment will affect the training response (*see* Fig. 40). Because all the energy pathways are being developed there will be some high-intensity work involved. The heart rate will fluctuate from 100 beats/min on the easy jog up to 180 on the long sustained bursts of 1km+. Like the alternating pace run, if done correctly this is bordering on a high-intensity type of training session. Similarly, it is a beneficial training method for improving maximum VO2 and, depending on the environment, the strength-endurance as well.

Repetition and interval training has a number of variables which are determined by the athlete's fitness and the time of year. This is a high-intensity type of training session, run at 100 per cent of the fitness level and will involve heart rates in the region of 165–180 beats/min. The variables associated with this particular type of session are the duration of each repetition/interval, the recovery between each, the type of recovery, the number of repetitions or sets, the intensity of the repetitions and the type of environment in which the training takes place. Because of these variables and how they are applied, there are a number of training effects. An overview of the variables is shown below (*see* Fig. 41).

• The *duration* of the repetitions can be either a distance, such as 200m intervals or 1-mile repetitions, or the repetition for a certain length of time. They will be of either short duration (15sec–2min),

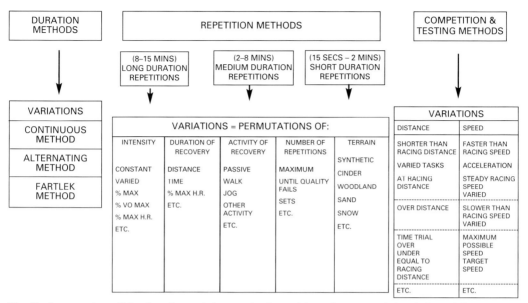

Fig.41. An overview of the duration training methods used in endurance training (adapted from Harre, 1973). The methods are covered in detail in this chapter.

medium duration (2–8min) or long duration (over 8min) (*see* Fig. 42).

- The *type of recovery* may be a timed recovery (half the time of the repetition), a jogged distance recovery (400m jog) or a pulse recovery (once the pulse returns 120 beats/min the athlete is ready to begin the next repetition).
- The *recovery* may be passive, sitting or lying down, a walk recovery, a jogged recovery or some other active recovery. The most effective and beneficial type of recovery is the jogged recovery as this allows the athlete to keep warm, get rid of waste products that have built up in the body and speed up recovery.
- The *number of repetitions and sets* used in any particular session will be determined by the fitness level, the time of year and the required effect of the session.
- The intensity of the session will be at a set, constant speed, a variable speed or at a set proportion of the maximum heart rate, fitness level or maximum volume oxygen uptake.

- These types of repetition session may be carried out on any t*ype of terrain*, such as a synthetic track, cinder track, woodland or forest path, parkland, golf course, sand or road.

The main aim of these types of session is to build up the athlete's aerobic base and maximum aerobic capacity.

Throughout the following pages the specimen training session examples will be indicated as follows: sets × repetitions (distance) (intensity or pace) (recovery between repetitions) and then (recovery between sets).

Three examples are:

i. 10 (repetitions) × 400 (m) in 60 (sec) with 2 (min recovery between each repetition)

ii. 3 (sets) × 4 (repetitions) × 300 (m) in 42 (sec) with 40 (sec between each repetition) and 5 (min between each set)

iii.2 (repetitions) × 500 (m) at (100% effort) with 8 (min recovery between repetitions) then 20 (min) recovery before 5

ENDURANCE TRAINING

Certain types of exercise and training will INCREASE certain bodily functions whilst others decrease them. The following is a look at these various methods, and their effects.

CHARACTERISTICS OF ENDURANCE

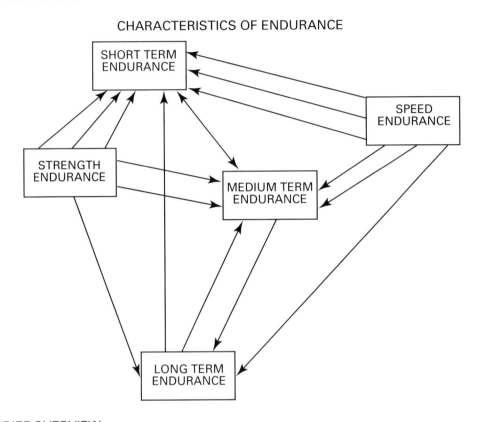

BRIEF OVERVIEW

1. Short Term Endurance (Aerobic) – 45 seconds to 2 minutes duration
2. Medium Term Endurance (Aerobic) – 2 to 8 minutes duration
3. Long Term Endurance (Aerobic) – 8 minutes plus
4. Speed Endurance (Anaerobic) – loads between 85%-100% maximum intensity
5. Strength Endurance (Anaerobic) – loads 4-6 x 25%-50% up to 3-5 x 50%-70%
6. Note the three Anaerobic Pathways – 5 seconds up to 2 minutes

Fig.42. A schematic diagram to show the interrelationship of the various aspects of endurance and their importance to each other. The more connections between them, the more interrelated and dependent they are on each other.

(repetitions) × 200 (m) in 27 (sec) with 2 (min recovery between each repetition)

The following are examples of how a repetition session, involving the same distance, may be progressed through the season. As the number of repetitions is increased and the recoveries are reduced the speed will remain constant, or increase due to the developing fitness level.

Late November during the mid-preparation phase:

5 × 1,000m, on grass, with 3min jog recovery, with the intensity at 100 per cent of fitness level.

Late January during the early part of the specific-preparation phase:

8 × 1,000m on grass, with 1min 30sec jog recovery, at 100 per cent intensity of fitness level.

Late March during the mid-specific-preparation phase:

2 × (5 × 1,000m) on grass with 1min 30sec jog recovery and 3min between sets, at 110 per cent of the fitness level.

Progressively improving the athlete's maximum volume oxygen uptake will also improve the function of the cardio-respiratory system and the capacity for aerobic work. Appropriate aerobic training will produce the following changes, which combine to improve maximum oxygen uptake:
- increased utilization of oxygen in and out of the lungs
- increased diffusion of oxygen from the lungs into the blood
- more efficient transport of oxygen by the blood
- more effective circulation of blood to the muscles

- an increased number and efficiency of capillaries
- an increased size and number of mitochondria
- an increased concentration and activity of aerobic enzymes.

Therefore the greater the amount of oxygen (maximum VO2) that can be utilized, the more efficient and effective he becomes. Females will have a maximum VO2 approximately 10 per cent lower than that of their male counterparts; this is due to the following factors involved in the transport and uptake of oxygen:

- smaller lung volume
- lower stroke volume
- smaller heart size
- lower blood volume
- lower levels of haemoglobin.

The three energy systems do not work independently. All the energy systems are active during exercise to a greater or lesser extent. In this context, the aerobic system uses oxygen to provide energy for the re-synthesis of ATP.

Alactate (ATP-CP) System

Training the ATP-CP system will involve maximum efforts of between 4 and 9sec in duration. This is because of the amount of ATP stored in the muscles and the amount that can be re-synthesized by utilizing the ATP-CP system. Therefore most of the training will involve maximum effort (100 per cent) within these time periods of 4–9sec or as part of a longer period where some of the running will be at sub-maximum level. This type of training is primarily to improve an athlete's pure speed and should always be done when he is fresh and with the focus on technique and relaxation. A good test of an athlete's speed and to see whether there has been an improvement when tested again is

Fig.43. Drills are essential in developing technique, coordination and relaxation. They can be done as either separate sessions or as dynamic stretching during warm-up. In this particular figure the athletes are performing a high knees exercise. The movement is done slowly to ensure that the correct technique is being used and that there is a high knee lift, driving off the toes and the rear foot and that the arms are active.

Fig.44. The side view shows the high knee lift, driving off the back foot, active arms and the head held erect, with the eyes looking straight ahead. This is the action that needs to be reproduced during the finish of a high-performance middle-distance race.

the 'flying speed' test. This is conducted over 40m from a standing start; times are taken at 20 and 40m to indicate how good is his acceleration. However, the key time is that taken between 20 and 40m, which is calculated by deducting one time from the other, and is called the flying 20m. This is because this 20m segment matches his maximum speed and is an indicator of sprinting ability relevant to his middle-distance event. The following are some of the methods which may be used to improve this energy system:

- sprint drills/dynamic stretching
- pure speed sprinting
- up the clock sessions
- down the clock sessions
- pyramid sessions
- downhill sprints
- acceleration sprints
- zigzag runs
- skills sprinting.

Sprint drills and dynamic stretching are a good introduction to training this energy system. They are both progressive, culminating in explosive movement over a short period. This type of training should be done at the start of the training session. As in all the training methods used for this energy system, an emphasis on technique is essential (*see* Fig. 43 to 48).

Fig.46. This drill would be included in a dynamic stretching programme. This is because the action is far more active and is done with a bounce. The drill requires a high knee drive, an active drive with a bounce off the rear leg and active arms. Research has shown that dynamic stretching prepares the athlete better for the demands of a high-intensity training session.

Fig.45. In this figure the athletes are extending their lead leg as far as possible. This action is also done very slowly, not only to give it extra emphasis but also to make the athlete more mobile through a greater range of movement and stronger in the pelvic area. All these drills will be over 20m, with three or four repetitions for each drill.

Pure speed sessions would start from either a rolling or a standing start over distances of 30 to 60m. The effort would be at maximum velocity, with a complete recovery between each repetition, a small number of repetitions in each set and a reasonable number of sets in total. This type of session should be done when the athlete is fresh and with an emphasis on technique and relaxation. An example of this type of session is as follows:

4 sets × 4 repetitions × 40m with 2–3min between repetitions and 8min between sets.

Fig.47. The athletes are shown bouncing and simultaneously driving off the ball of the rear foot, the high knee action working in unison with the active arms. The dynamic stretching drills are good for developing and moulding good technique. They should be carried out over distances varying from 10 to 30m and are excellent preparation for the main focus of the training session. However, the drills must be progressed through walking, hopping and skipping to thoroughly warm up the body and ensure that there is no chance of injury.

Fig.48. With this drill, commonly called 'heel' flicks, the emphasis is on working the legs as quickly as possible. The rear leg works actively behind the standing leg to try and touch the athlete's bottom and then the legs change places. The idea is to have as many heel flicks as possible in the 10 or 20m duration of the drill. A slight forward lean will help the athlete. This drill is good for working the gluteus muscles and assisting with leg cadence.

An *up the clock* session again would be run at maximum velocity, with a complete recovery between each repetition and would progress as follows:

30m/40m/50m/60m/70m/80m, 2–3min between each repetition.

A *down the clock* session would be exactly the same session in reverse, but culminating with the shortest sprint. If more than one set of either the up the clock or the down the clock session is undertaken, there should be at least 8–10min between sets:

80m/70m/60m/50m/40m/30m, with 2–3min between each repetition.

A *pyramid training* session would begin with the shortest sprint and progress to the longest before returning to the shortest. As in each of the other activities, the repetitions should be run at maximum velocity with the emphasis on technique and relaxation and a complete recovery between each repetition and each set. A typical example of a pyramid session would be as follows:

30m→40m→50m→60m→50m→40m→ 30m, with 3min recovery between each repetition.

To improve leg cadence it is occasionally worth doing a *downhill training* session. This type of session should be done on grass, with a downhill gradient of no more than 10 degrees over distances ranging from 30 to 80m, with a complete recovery in between each repetition. The idea is to get the legs moving much more quickly than would be achieved on a straight surface. However, care must be taken with both technique and safety to ensure that the runner does not overbalance.

Acceleration sprints are an essential part of the middle-distance runner's equipment. There are different methods in which acceleration can be included in the training sessions to replicate the race situation. The following two examples of skills sprinting are methods that can be adopted to improve the ATP-CP system and also the runner's ability

marathon pace	5k/10k pace	800m/1,500m pace	400m pace	sprint pace
30m→	60m→	90m→	120m→	150m→

Fig.48a.

to accelerate. To get a feel for how acceleration is occurring, a distance of 150m is ideal, with a complete recovery between each repetition and up to six to eight repetitions in total. The 150m would be broken down into 30m segments, and the pace would accelerate as follows: the first 30m would be run at marathon pace, the next segment at the long-distance pace, the third segment at the 800/1,500m pace, the fourth at 400m pace, and the final segment at sprint pace (*see* Fig. 48a).

Even though the training duration is longer than the time it takes to break down the ATP-CP system, this happens only in the final 30m, between 120 and 150m, since this is the only segment where the runner will be operating at maximum velocity.

A similar type of training method to improve acceleration would be to stride at sub-maximum pace around the track and, on a given command or whistle blast, react by accelerating for 60m. The number of repetitions would be quite low at from four to six, with a complete recovery between each.

Zigzag runs may be either a speed and acceleration drill or a strength-endurance training session (*see* Chapter 4). A series of six markers (*see* Fig. 49) are placed at 30m intervals in a zigzag pattern. Six 30m sprints are made with five 90-degree turns around each marker. Because the athlete has to decelerate round each marker and then accelerate to the next, this improves both his coordination and his ability to accelerate. There would be only a few repetitions in each set, about four or five, and two to three sets with a walk back recovery between each repetition and complete recovery between sets. This is to ensure that he can run at

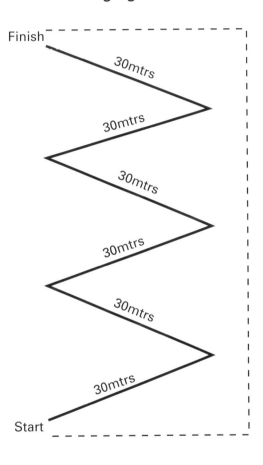

Zigzag Run

Finish

30mtrs

30mtrs

30mtrs

30mtrs

30mtrs

30mtrs

Start

– – – – – Jogged recovery run

Fig.49. A diagram to show how the zigzag training drill is set out. This particular exercise can be used as either an acceleration drill, a speed drill or a strength-endurance drill. The dotted line denotes the recovery, the length of which will vary according to the required effect, as will the total number of sets and repetitions.

maximum intensity for each of the repetitions.

Skills sprinting (*see* Fig. 49a below) is intended to get him to replicate possible race situations and to work on his acceleration and ATP-CP system. The training distance would be 60m, split into three segments of 20m. With this type of training to cover all the racing requirements there are four sets with three repetitions in each, 2min between each repetition and about 8–10min between sets. The first is progressive acceleration through each of the three segments, the second set is at maximum speed for the first segment, then 90 per cent effort for the second segment before returning to maximum speed for the final segment. The third set is at 95 per cent effort for the first segment, followed by maximum speed for the second segment and a controlled 95 per cent for the final one. This has to be controlled since the temptation is to ease off too much and not run at the required speed. The final set is at maximum velocity throughout the three segments for the whole 60m.

All of the methods mentioned can be performed over slightly longer distances, ranging from 80 to 150m. However, this will then involve the anaerobic energy pathway and would not be a pure speed training session because of the duration involved and the intensity of the repetition, but would also involve some speed-endurance training. This type of session may be used if a combination of both the energy pathways is required for the training programme.

Middle-distance runners often neglect these types of training session. The key is working at maximum intensity for between 4 and 9sec and ensuring that the recovery is adequate enough to allow for the full re-synthesis of the system, so that high-intensity levels can be maintained. It is important that both the correct recovery and adequate warm-up and cool-down are allowed for; this is because with this type of training there is a high demand on the muscles and a relative high potential for injury. The aim of these sessions is not only to improve and maintain maximum speed, employing good technique and relaxation, but also to improve the ability to react, adjust and accelerate, as well as limiting the effects of the endurance factors.

Set 1

80% velocity	90% velocity	100% velocity
20m→	40m→	60m→

Set 2

100% velocity	90% velocity	100 % velocity
20m→	40m→	60m→

Set 3

95% velocity	100% velocity	95% velocity
20m→	40m→	60m→

Set 4

100% velocity	100% velocity	100% velocity
20m→	40m→	60m→

Fig. 49a Skills Spinting.

Anaerobic (Lactate) System

This system is very important for middle-distance runners as it makes a significant contribution during short-term and maximum efforts. It is often referred to as speed-endurance training and is the predominant supplier of ATP during efforts lasting up to 45sec and also up to 2min where the aerobic system has an increasing input. Therefore the middle-distance runner's training should include work in the range of 10sec to 2min duration at high intensity. During this type of training the body develops a tolerance to the build-up of lactate in the blood. At rest, lactate levels are about 1 millimole per litre (mmol/ltr) of blood and can rise to values in excess of 25 mmol/ltr during intense exercise. There is a point, as the intensity increases, where there is a rapid increase in the level of blood lactate. This is referred to as the *onset of blood lactate accumulation* (OBLA). Blood lactate accumulation is the lactate that builds up in the blood, minus that which the athlete is able to remove from the blood. Once this point is reached, it is referred to as the lactate threshold. To determine this blood samples can be taken by an exercise physiologist during high-intensity training sessions. However, to get the most valid results these samples should be taken at critical times during the training and at a predetermined time after the end of it. The lactate threshold is usually expressed as a percentage of the maximum VO2. With training, the lactate threshold level can be improved because training has improved the efficiency of lactate removal. In high-performance athletes their lactate threshold will be as high as 70–80 per cent of their maximum VO2. The lactate threshold is a good indicator of performance: if two athletes have a similar maximum VO2, it is usually the one with the higher lactate threshold (OBLA) who will produce the better performance. High-performance 800m runners will be performing at levels of 20+ mmol/ltr of blood lactate, and a 1,500m runner at 18 mmol/ltr of blood lactate. Therefore high-performance middle-distance runners need to consider training methods which will raise their lactate threshold to improve their performance, as well as training to raise their maximum VO2. When doing anaerobic repetition work, it is essential that the athlete remains relaxed and concentrates on his technique. This type of training session is highly specific to the athlete and therefore group training is not recommended. This is because each training programme should be tailored to each individual and only one of the group would get the maximum benefit from this specific training session.

The following are some of the types of training which are used to train and develop this energy pathway:

- quality repetitions
- pyramids
- up the clock session
- down the clock session
- differentials/split intervals
- pace injectors
- tired surges
- pace increases
- high-intensity repetitions
- time trials.

Some of the following sessions are similar to those previously mentioned, but will differ in the duration of the repetition, the number of repetitions and the length of the recovery period. The key to training the lactate system is to run a small number of repetitions at maximum speed, with a sufficiently long recovery to maintain quality. With all the following lactate (speed-endurance) sessions the heart rates will be over 170 and up to 200+ beats/min. This is because this type of training is anaerobic. A *quality repetition* session for a female 1,500m runner with a personal best of

4.00min would be as follows:

3 × 500m in 76sec (faster than the race pace of 80sec) with a 4–5min recovery between repetitions;

2 × 1,000m in 2min 35sec with a 15min recovery between the repetitions.

This type of training will help the body's adaptation to both the speed of the repetition and the build-up of lactic acid in the system.

A *pyramid training* session to train the lactate system or for speed-endurance would involve longer distance repetitions with longer recoveries. There will be few repetitions involved with their being run at faster than race pace. Using the same 4.00min, 1,500m female runner a typical pyramid session would be as shown in Fig.49b.

With the up and down the clock sessions it would again involve longer repetitions in duration and fewer repetitions in total with long recoveries. Examples of both these types of training sessions are shown in Fig. 49c.

Both these sessions are structured to ensure that the body develops a tolerance against the build up of lactic acid. Of the two, the down the clock session is slightly easier both physiologically and mentally because the distance at each repetition is diminishing as the session progresses. Whereas with the up the clock session, as the body gets more fatigued and there is a build up of lactic acid, the repetitions become progressively longer.

Differentials or *split intervals* are used to improve both speed-endurance and pace judgement. With these sessions the repetition is split into two and both sections are either run at the same pace or the second section is made slightly faster. To help with his pace judgement, the coach may use a whistle to signal when the target time has elapsed. The following is an example of how the session could be run with the second part of the repetition run quicker for a 3min, 34sec male 1,500m runner.

Differential/Split interval:
4 × 400m in 55sec, the first 200m in 28.5sec, the second 200m in 26.5sec with 5–6min recovery between each repetition.

Pace injectors, tired surges and *pace increases* are not only speed-endurance sessions which train the anaerobic lactate system, they are also excellent sessions both in simulating race situations and improving acceleration. The following are examples of these three types of training session.

200m (30sec)/300m (46sec)/400m (62sec)/300m (46sec)/200m (30sec)
Recovery: 3min   4min   5min   4min

Fig 49b Pyramid training.

Up the Clock:
200m (30sec)→300m (46sec)→ 400m (62sec)→ 500m (78sec)→ 600m (94sec)
Recovery: 2min   4min   6min   8min

Down the Clock:
600m (94sec)→ 500m (78sec)→ 400m (62sec)→ 300m (46sec)→ 200m (30sec)
Recovery: 8min   6min   4min   2min

Fig 49c Up and down the clock training.

Pace injectors:
4 × 600m with 8min recovery between each repetition.

Race pace of 1min 56sec for a female 800m runner.

The three 200m sections broken down as follows: first 200m, 29sec (race pace); second 200m, 26sec; third 200m, 29sec (race pace).

Tired surges:
3 × 500m/200m, with 100m jog between each repetition and 8–10min recovery between each set; race pace of 3min 34sec for a male 1,500m runner.

500m in 70sec (faster than race pace), jog 100m 200m in 27.5sec (faster than race pace).

Pace increases:
3 × 900m with 10–12min recovery between each repetition.

First 300m in 43sec (race pace), second 300m in 41sec, third 300m in 39sec.

Each of these sessions will help the athlete to cope with the race situation: the pace injectors prepare him physically to be able to react to any sudden injection of pace; the pace increases prepare him for making a long sustained run to the finish, if this is what is required; and the tired surges simulate the conclusion of the race, since there will still be some lactic acid in the legs which the 100m jog will not have had time to disperse.

The *high-intensity repetitions* are to be used only with mature, high-performance athletes. The aim here is get the athlete to run repetitions at a high intensity when there is lactic acid still in his system. The repetitions are run at maximum intensity, with a short recovery between the repetitions, and a longer recovery between the sets. With this particular type of training there is a high concentration of lactate in the system and the pulse rate could be as high as 190 to 200 beats/min. The distances which are most effective for this session are 200 or 300m; the following example is a combination of both distances for an 800m runner with a personal best of 1min 44sec:

3 × (300m/200m) 20sec between each repetition and 8min between sets.

The 300m would be run in 38sec (faster than race pace) and the 200m in 25–26sec (faster than race pace).

Time trials and *tests* should be used sparingly and at particular stages of the training programme. They are used as an indicator of how the training has progressed. However, the phase of the training, the weather and the athlete's health should be taken into consideration when undertaking them. Because they are run at maximum effort, the time trials are a good indicator of race speed at this particular time. Most time trials are not over the race distance but either under or over it. A 1,500m runner may therefore have a time trial in the pre-competition phase over 2,000 or 3,000m to check on his endurance. To gauge how his speed-endurance is progressing, he may test himself over 1,000m at the start of the competition phase. Similarly, the 800m runner would use distances of 1,000 or 1,200m to check the progress of his endurance and a 600m time trial to see how his speed-endurance is progressing.

Assessments which can also be used to measure fitness at both 800 and 1,500m are the Kosmin tests. The 800m runner would run as far as he could on the track in 60sec; after a 3min rest he would repeat the 60sec run and add the distance covered in the two repetitions together. The total distance is then referred to a chart (*see* Fig. 50 and 51) to indicate the time expected in a competition; for example, if the total covered was 940m a time of 1min 45.4sec would be expected in competition. The 1,500m runner would run 4 × 60sec as hard

The Kosmin Test for Event-Specific Endurance (800m)

The athlete runs for 60sec with the distance covered being measure and recorded, The runner takes 3 minutes rest and runs again for 60sec. After adding the two distances covered, the time to be expected in competition can be seen in the following tables:

Distance	Expected Time	Distance	Expected Time	Distance	Expected Time
500	2:38.0	655	2:19.5	805	2:01.6
505	2:37.4	660	2:18.9	810	2:01.0
510	2:36.8	665	2:19.3	815	2:00.4
515	2:26.2	670	2:17.7	820	1:59.8
520	2:35.0	675	2:17.1	825	1:59.2
525	2:35.0	680	2: 16.5	830	1:58.6
535	2:33.8	685	2: 15.9	835	1:58.0
540	2:33.2	690	2: 15.3	840	1:57.4
545	2:32.6	695	2: 14.7	845	1:56.8
550	2:32.0	700	2: 14.1	850	1:56.2
555	2:31.4	705	2: 16.5	855	1:55.7
560	2:30.8	710	2: 12.9	860	1:55.1
565	2:30.2	715	2:12.3	865	1:54.5
570	2:29.6	720	2:11.7	870	1:53.9
575	2:29.0	725	2:11.1	875	1:53.3
580	2:28.4	730	2:10.5	880	1:52.7
585	2:27.8	735	2:09.9	885	1:52.2
590	2:27.2	740	2:09.4	890	1:51.5
595	2:26.6	745	2: 08.8	895	1:50.9
600	2:26.0	750	2: 08.2	900	1:50.3
605	2:25.4	755	2: 07.6	905	1:49.7
610	2:24.8	760	2: 07.0	910	1:49.1
615	2:24.2	765	2: 06.4	915	1:48.5
620	2:23.6	770	2: 05.8	920	1:47.9
625	2:23.0	775	2: 05.2	925	1:47.3
630	2:22.4	780	2:04.6	930	1:46.6
635	2:21.8	785	2: 04.0	935	1:46.0
640	2:21.2	790	2:03.4	940	1:45.4
645	2:20.6	795	2:02.8	945	1:44.8
650	2:20.1	800	2:02.2	950	1:44.2

Fig.50. Chart to show the Kosmin test for predicting 800m potential.

The Kosmin Test for Event-Specific Endurance (1500m)

The athlete runs for 4 x 60sec with a rest of 3 minutes after the first run, 2 minutes after the second run and 1 minute after the third run. The distances covered in each run are summed. The time to be expected in competition can be seen in the following tables:

Distance	Expected Time	Distance	Expected Time	Distance	Expected Time
1300	4:49.7	1455	4:24.6	1610	3:59.5
1305	4:48.9	1460	4:23.8	1615	3:58.7
1310	4:48.1	1465	4:22.9	1620	3:57.9
1315	4:47.3	1470	4:22.1	1625	3:57.1
1320	4:46.5	1475	4:21.3	1630	3:56.3
1325	4:45.6	1480	4:20.4	1635	3:55.4
1330	4:44.8	1485	4:19.7	1640	3:54.6
1335	4:44.0	1490	4:18.9	1645	3:53.8
1340	4:43.2	1495	4:18.1	1650	3:53.0
1345	4:42.4	1500	4:17.3	1655	3:52.2
1350	4:41.6	1505	4:16.5	1660	3:51.4
1355	4:40.8	1510	4:15.7	1665	3:50.6
1360	4:40.0	1515	4:14.9	1670	3:49.7
1365	4:39.2	1520	4:14.1	1675	3:48.9
1370	4:38.4	1525	4:13.2	1680	3:48.1
1375	4:37.5	1530	4:12.4	1685	3:47.3
1380	4:36.7	1535	4:11.6	1690	3:46.5
1385	4:35.9	1540	4:10.8	1695	3:45.7
1390	4:35.1	1545	4:10.0	1700	3:44.9
1395	4:34.3	1550	4:09.2	1705	3:44.1
1400	4:33.5	1555	4:08.4	1710	3:43.2
1405	4:32.7	1560	4:07.6	1715	3:42.4
1410	4:31.9	1565	4:06.8	1720	3:41.6
1415	4:31.1	1570	4:05.9	1725	3:40.8
1420	4:30.3	1575	4:05.1	1730	3:40.0
1425	4:29.5	1580	4:04.3	1735	3:39.2
1430	4:28.7	1585	4:03.5	1740	3:38.4
1435	4:27.8	1590	4:02.7	1745	3:37.6
1440	4:27.0	1595	4:01.9	1750	3:36.7
1445	4:26.2	1600	4:01.1	1755	3:35.9
1450	4:25.4	1605	4:00.3		

Fig.51. Chart to show the Kosmin test for predicting 1,500m potential.

as possible, with a rest of 3min after the first run, 2min after the second and 1min after the third. The distances covered in each of the four repetitions are added together and the total is referred to a chart to ascertain his expected time in competition; for example, if the total covered in the four repetitions was 1,610m the expected time in the competition would be 3min 59.5sec.

All these training sessions are designed to train the energy pathways and make them more efficient in competitive running. Within each of the three energy pathways there is a great deal of variety, race simulation and an overlapping of each of the pathways which are performing at different levels depending on the type of training session. It is essential that the intensities and progressions are correct. Fig. 52 shows how the repetitions and intensities should be developed.

Once the types of training described above have taken place, it is important that during the pre-competition phase, and particularly during the competition phase, that event-specific training takes place a minimum of once a week. This type of training is a mixture of the other three types and therefore there are elements of alactate, lactate and aerobic training involved. This is because event-specific training is the

Progression of Repetitions

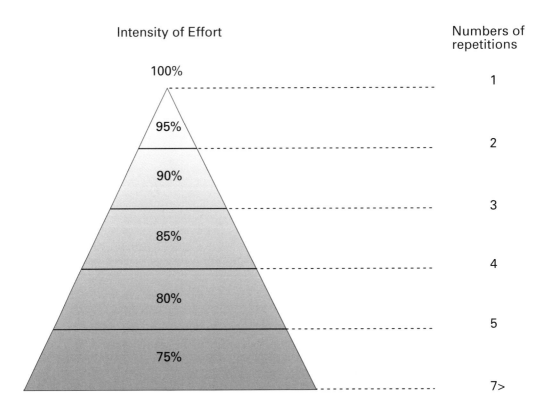

Fig.52. Overview of how repetitions should be progressed with regard to loading and intensity. This is applicable to both endurance training and weight training.

culmination of the year's training and also simulates the race's requirements. Event-specific training has three key areas: the total of the two sets is always the race distance, the second set repetitions are always shorter, and every repetition in each set should be at race pace. Therefore a male 1,500m runner aiming to run 3min 30sec would undertake the following event-specific session with all the repetitions run at race pace:

500m (70sec) 1min recovery, 700m (98sec) 30sec recovery, 300m (42sec) 15–20min recovery
5 × 300m (42sec) 1min recovery between repetitions.

It is important that all the energy pathways are trained and at the correct stage of the year. Progression is the key throughout the year and the repetitions should be progressed as indicated in Fig.52 so that they move from being aerobic-based in the preparation phases to becoming far more anaerobic and event-specific in the competition phases. This means that, as the season progresses, quantity is replaced by quality, short recoveries by complete recoveries and low-intensity training by maximum-intensity training. The following chart (Fig. 53) shows the different types of interval (repetition) method and their training effect. The first of the following two figures (Fig. 53a) shows how the three energy systems are developed through training at the correct intensity and with the correct recoveries. The second figure (Fig. 54) is a summary of the interrelationship of the three energy systems and how the training methods affect their development.

Method	Quantity	Recovery	Intensity/lactate level	Aim
extensive interval	15–20	1min 30sec	low (4–8)	general endurance
intensive interval	2 sets of 4	3–7min	medium (8–12)	speed-endurance
repetition method	2 sets of 2	7–15min	high (12–18)	specific speed-endurance
competition method	2	complete	maximum (20–25)	event-specific

Fig. 53

DEVELOPMENT OF THE THREE ENERGY SYSTEMS

	Anaerobic Alactic	Anaerobic Lactic	Aerobic
Duration	0 – 8 secs	8 secs – 1 min	1 – 60 mins +
Distance	20m – 80m	80m – 400m	300m – 15Km or continuous runs
Intensity	maximal	90% - 100%	50% - 85%
Repetitions	3 – 4	1 – 5	3 – 20
Recovery	1 – 3 mins	2 – 10 mins	1 – 3 mins
Sets	1 – 4	1 – 4	1 – 4
Recovery	8 – 10 mins	10 – 20 mins	5 – 8 mins

Fig.53a. This table shows the development of the three energy systems used in endurance training. The required duration, intensity and numbers of sets, repetitions and recoveries for the three are detailed.

Running Terms	Speed	Speed Endurance	Intensive Repetitions	Extensive Repetitions	Continuous
Contribution of the Energy Systems	ATP-CP System	Anaerobic Lactic System			Aerobic System
Intensity	95% – 105%	95% – 100%	80% – 90%	60% – 80%	40% – 60%
Distance of Run	20m–60m	60m – 600m	up to 1200m	up to 1200m plus up to 500m Continuous	5000m+
No of reps/set	3 – 4	1 – 5	3 – 12	6 – 30	–
No of sets	3 – 5 (5)	0 – 3	1 – 3	1 – 3	1
Total distance of sets	80m – 120m				
Total dist. in session	200m – 600m	300m – 1800m	Long	Long	–
Recovery/reps	[2′ – 3′]	Incomplete, Nearly Complete and Complete [2′ – 20′]	pulse 50–60% max [3′ – 5′]	pulse 60–70% max [1′ – 3′]	–
Recovery/sets	[8 – 10′]	[8′ – 10′]	Nearly complete [7′ – 20′]	Incomplete [5′ – 7′]	–

Fig.54. Summary of the interrelationships of the three energy systems and the running activities in their development. The loading and intensities should always be relevant to the individual athlete, his age and the time of the season (after B. Mcfarlane, 1988).

CHAPTER 4
Conditioning Training

Success in a major middle-distance championship competition can be determined by how strong an athlete remains during four rounds of competition. Strength training through conditioning can greatly enhance both an athlete's training programme and his ability to compete at the highest level. Strength and conditioning training falls into four major categories: gross strength, elastic strength (also known as power, fast strength or strength at speed), strength endurance and resistance training. The high-performance middle-distance runner will use all these types of strength and conditioning, but some more than others. When using weight training as a conditioning session the same principle with the number of repetitions and the level of intensity applies as with repetition running training (*see* Fig. 52).

GROSS STRENGTH

The area of strength training which is used least by middle-distance runners is gross

Fig.55. The squat exercise is good for all-round strengthening and conditioning. However, care must be taken with safety and the correct technique used. This exercise helps the balance of the body since it uses the major muscle groups of the legs in the correct order and at the correct time (gluteus/hamstrings/quadriceps). The back should be kept straight, eyes looking ahead and the knees bent to, or just below, the horizontal. If the back and the upper body are weak, this leads in a race to the shoulders' lifting and tightening. To address and strengthen this area, the bar may be held above the head not on the shoulders. If the athlete is not strong enough to do this he can start without a bar, use a towel or broom handle and go through the full movement. When the exercise is performed completely in this way it strengthens the whole core of the body.

Fig.56. This exercise is to strengthen the calves. The weight is across the shoulders and the heels are then raised off the ground, with the balls of the feet and toes taking the weight through the calf area. The key to this exercise is to ensure that the poundage is correct and that the position is not held for too long, putting too much weight on the calves. Photo: Spencer G. Duval

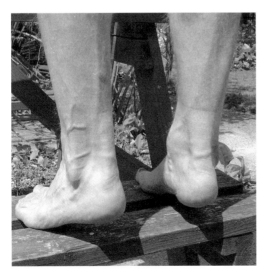

Fig.56a.(left) This close-up shows the same exercise on a bench without any weights being carried on the shoulders. A similar exercise to strengthen the hip area is to stand on a single leg with the other straight ahead and for the stationary leg to be lowered as slowly and as low as possible. The athlete, to avoid over-balancing at first, may need support by putting one hand on a wall or other stationary object. Photo: Spencer G. Duval

Fig.56b (above). This step-up exercise can be performed on to as low an object as a telephone directory and then progressed to a box top. The correct poundage should be used to avoid any injuries. The hips are kept low, with the weight going over the front foot, not the back foot, when the step-up takes place. It is an active exercise which strengthens the quadriceps. Photo: Spencer G. Duval

Fig.57. The lunge exercise, like the squat exercise, is a good all-round one, strengthening the correct muscles in the correct order and at the correct time (gluteus→hamstrings→quadriceps). The athlete should have his eyes looking forwards, the hips square, a straight back and a foot extended to the front. Photo: Spencer G. Duval

Fig.57a. The side shot of the lunge shows how the knee is not rotating inwards, outwards nor is it too far forward. As with the squat exercise, the bar can be lifted above the head with the arms apart. This not only strengthens the chest and the upper back but also improves an athlete's capacity to breathe. If the bar is too heavy it may be replaced initially by a broom or a towel. The lunge exercise can also be a dynamic exercise with the athlete's walking into the lunge positions with the bar above his head. Photo: Spencer G. Duval

strength training (often referred to as maximum strength training). This type of training is defined as developing the greatest force the neuromuscular system is capable of exerting in a single contraction. With this type of training free weights are used predominantly, with the occasional use of machines. Therefore the force lifted is of a high resistance and weight and the number of repetitions is low. The loading therefore will be in the range of 90 to 100 per cent of the maximum lift, with few repetitions and a higher number of sets (for example, bench press: 8 sets × 2 lifts × 95 per cent loading). Most of the exercises used in any form of weight training should be predominantly for the legs (*see* Fig. 55–57 for examples). The effect of this type of training is to increase muscle bulk; it therefore slows movements and has little effect on fast strength. From the middle-distance runner's perspective this type of training is best used in rehabilitation after injury and to eradicate any areas of weakness.

Because this type of training is carried out with free weights it is of paramount importance that the lifter's technique is correct in order to avoid any injury; similarly, he should be accompanied by 'spotters' on either side when undertaking a lifting session to ensure that the weighted bar is not dropped, again risking injury.

Fig.59. Looking at Fig.58 from the side shows the driving action of the arms and the full extension of the rear leg. As well as strengthening the natural running action this exercise also strengthens the biceps muscles (agonist muscle).

Fig.58. Too many drills or weight training activities are not event-specific and therefore have little benefit. With this exercise the athlete is simulating the running action using dumbbells. The hands are up at eye level, the elbows at 90 degrees and the feet in the running position.

As with other types of strength training, it is important that each activity is compensated for by the next. This means that if the first exercise involves strengthening the active muscle, known as the agonist, the following one will be to strengthen its partner support muscle, known as the antagonist. For example, in an exercise activating the hamstring muscles (agonist), its partner support muscle, the

Fig.60. Having worked the biceps muscles in the previous exercise, the next one is to strengthen the partner muscle, the antagonist muscle, which is the triceps. With this action the feet are in the running position and the arms pump the dumb-bells in the air above the head.

Fig.61. Like the previous exercise for the biceps muscles this action is done vigorously for the duration of the exercise. When it is repeated the legs change position. This exercise also helps to strengthen the chest and the upper back area.

quadriceps (antagonist) should be also strengthened. Whichever muscles are being strengthened a team of muscles called synergist muscles will be supporting them.

All muscles depending on the exercise involved can either be active (agonist) or a partner support muscle (antagonist) (*see* Fig. 58–61).

Fig.63. In this figure the athlete is in the landing phase (the take-off phase is similar), her knees are bent to help to cushion the landing. The hurdles should always be placed at the appropriate height and distance for the athlete.

Fig.62. A row of hurdles can be used for plyometric exercises or depth jumps. This type of training should be done only with a mature athlete, on a soft surface and under supervision. In this figure the athlete is coming out of the take-off position with a double arm action, driving off on her toes as she jumps over the hurdle double-footed.

ELASTIC STRENGTH

This is the ability of the neuromuscular system to overcome resistance with a high speed of contraction. Often referred to, as we have noted, as power, fast strength or strength at speed, this type of training aids performance in the explosive events. Here again free weights would be predominantly used with a loading of 75 to 85 per cent of the maximum. The lifts are done faster than with maximum strength lifting, but the same rules of technique, safety and the use of spotters apply. The number of repetitions will vary from six to ten, with the number of sets being three or four, with short recoveries between sets. The effect of this type of training is some bulking of the muscle and increase in contractile speed. Elastic strength training not only underpins the other aspects of the training programme but it is also beneficial in shorter endurance events, particularly with the assistance of acceleration.

One aspect of elastic strength is *plyometric* training. With this method, hopping, skipping and bounding are incorporated into the training programme. Similarly, medicine ball

Fig.64. Medicine ball exercises are recommended for both coordination and for strength-endurance work. The number of repetitions, the number of drills, the distance between the athletes and the weights of the balls should be applicable to the athlete's ability. In this series of exercises the athletes are using a basketball chest pass technique with the medicine ball. The athlete with the ball will release it to the other who will receive it and return it.

Fig.65. The same activity is progressed so that the athletes are kneeling. This means that they cannot use their legs and so their arms and abdominal muscles are strengthened. The distance between them may have to be shortened.

Fig.66. The athletes would then progress to sitting with their legs apart, again working on their arms and abdominal muscles. In this figure they are in the start position for the fourth of the series of exercises which involves lying on the back.

Fig.67. From the position in Fig.66 the athletes sit upright and, as they reach the vertical position, they release the medicine ball as a chest pass. The receiver catches the ball and the momentum allows them to fall backwards into the start position shown in Fig.66, and the exercise is continued. This exercise requires good abdominal strength and mobility.

Fig.69. The same exercise but this time without the legs as a driving force. The arms are still extended and this again puts even more emphasis on the back, chest and abdominal muscles. The action is the same as in Fig.68.

Fig.68. In this medicine ball activity the athletes are the optimal distance apart. The athlete has extended the ball above her head to release it from this position. This strengthens and stretches the arms, the front of the chest and the upper back. The legs are apart and the ball is then released and caught at a similar height by the opposite athlete.

Fig.70. The third of the extended arm exercises involves sitting with legs apart, putting even more emphasis on the arms, chest, back and abdominal muscles. This figure shows the start of the fourth exercise with the athlete lying on her back with arms extended. She then sits up releasing the ball, still with extended arms, as she reaches the vertical position.

Fig.71. This figure shows the athlete in the sitting up position about to release the ball. The receiving athlete catches the ball at its highest point and allows the momentum to take her into the start position in Fig.70. The exercise is then repeated. This exercise again isolates the chest, back and abdominal muscles. The stronger and more open the chest area the better it helps the athlete to breathe. There are a variety of similar exercises using medicine balls and for each of them the progression from standing, to kneeling, to sitting and to the lying position would apply. The number of repetitions is dependent on the ability of the athletes.

work and hurdle jumping are integral parts of plyometric training (*see* Fig. 62–71), and the mature athlete may also include depth jumping. These activities involve jumping off benches and gymnastic half and full boxes. The landing surface needs to be cushioned to avoid injury. The effects of plyometric training are that it improves the speed of muscle contraction, elastic strength and can aid speed-endurance. It is beneficial for middle-distance runners, but must follow other forms of strength training. It is advisable with plyometric and bounding exercises to ensure that they are done on a soft, forgiving surface such as grass, parkland or golf courses. Plyometric training can be incorporated in an athlete's training programme from an early age, whereas bounding should be introduced with only the mature athlete who is strong enough to cope with it.

STRENGTH ENDURANCE

This type of training involves lighter weights, either free or with machines, with a loading of 60 to 75 per cent of his maximum lift, but may also be included in running training and circuit training. The methods will vary, depending on the required training effect. The effect of this type of training is to increase muscular endurance, which may be either general or specific. It is appropriate for all endurance events and could be used for general, all-round conditioning or be specific to certain aspects such as speed. The effect of strength-endurance training is to ensure that the muscles continue to perform at the same rate even though they become fatigued.

Circuit Training

Circuit and stage training may also be either general or specific. The following examples show a general conditioning circuit used to develop overall, general conditioning during the general preparation phase. A far more specific circuit will replace this during the specific preparation phase. However, to get the maximum benefits for his athlete, the coach should design an individual circuit for him which is linked to his needs. The types of exercise of arms, legs and abdomen and general ones are shown in the illustrations, as are the number of circuits and the times and recoveries for each exercise. The exercises involved are as follows:

- chins on a gymnastic beam, either under-grasp or the more difficult over-grasp; the athlete raises himself up, using his arms until his chin is above the beam, he then lowers himself and repeats (arms);
- step ups onto one bench and then with the other foot onto a second bench, two benches high, reverse back down to the second bench and then the floor and repeat (legs);
- chinnies, a type of sit-up where, as the athlete sits up, he twists his body so that one knee is touched by his opposite elbow, the hands are clasped behind the head; he then returns to the prone position and repeats the exercise (abdominal) (Fig. 72);
- star jumps: squatting, hands between feet, spring up with legs apart, return to the start position and repeat (general) (Fig. 73);
- press ups (arms);
- jumping to touch a gymnastic beam placed at an appropriate height; as soon as he lands, he bounces back up to touch the beam repeatedly (legs);
- inclined sit ups, with the feet attached to a bench which is fastened to the gymnasium wall bars at a suitable angle, the hands clasped behind the head (abdominal);
- burpees start from a press-up position, then the legs come forward towards the arms; at this point he jumps up into the air as high as possible; when he lands he shoots his legs back into the starting press-up position and repeats the exercise (general);
- rope climb to the top of the gymnasium with either a double rope, using both arms only with no assistance from the legs or with a single rope and using the arms and feet (arms) (Fig. 74);
- bent knee sit-ups, but, instead of starting from a prone position, the exercise starts with the knees bent and the body moving from the floor to the knees and returning to the floor before repeating the exercise, the hands clasped behind the head (abdominal);
- shuttle run: fetching, carrying and returning two medicine balls in turn over a set distance (legs);
- star jumps: as previously, but with legs split one in front of the other (general) (Fig. 75 and 76);
- tricep dips either on the parallel bars or on a single bench; the arms are at full extension and then lowered to a 90-degree angle and held; the athlete then returns to the full extension position and repeats the exercise (arms) (Fig. 80–1);
- jumping over a row of hurdles, either with a single- or double-footed take-off or a mixture of both; it is essential that the hurdles be on gymnastic mats to avoid any impact injuries (legs) (as in Fig. 62 and 63);
- leg raises: lying flat on the back, arms at the side with the legs held together 15cm off the floor for the whole of the allotted time (abdominal);
- beam traverse: hanging from a gymnasium beam, the athlete moves along it, one arm following the other until the far end is reached and then returning using the arms only (arms);
- squat thrusts: in a press-up position, both legs move to the arms and then back to the starting position repeatedly (legs) (Fig. 77 and 78);
- bench jumps holding a medicine ball: with a leg on either side of the bench, jump up on to the bench with both feet and then back to the floor and continue to repeat the exercise (general).

Another general activity, not included in this particular circuit, is bench raises: the bench is hooked onto the wall bar at the

Fig.72. Chinnies is an exercise used to strengthen the abdominal area. It starts like a normal sit-up in the horizontal position with the arms behind the head. However, unlike a normal sit up, when the upright position is reached the body is twisted so that the opposite knee touches the opposite elbow and then returns to the horizontal position. On the next sit-up the other elbow touches the opposite knee and so on.

Fig.73. (above) There are two types of exercise called star-jumps which are used as general conditioning exercises. In this one the athlete starts in a crouched position, hands between the legs and the head upright. The athlete then springs into the air as high as possible to achieve the position shown here. He then returns to the start position and repeats.

Fig.74. (right) The rope climb exercise in a gymnastic circuit can be used on a single rope by using just the arms or with the addition of the legs to move up the rope. In this particular exercise the athlete is using two ropes and the arms only. Both exercises are for the arms, but this particular exercise also requires strong abdominals. Once the top is reached he returns to the bottom of the rope and repeats the exercise until it is completed.

Fig.75. This figure shows the starting position for the second type of star-jump, the split-star jump which is a general endurance exercise but also has an effect upon the legs.

Fig.76. (bottom left) From the start position in Fig.75 the athlete springs as high as possible into the air. While in the air the legs change position. When he lands, therefore, the legs are in the opposite positions from the start of the exercise and are ready to begin the next split star-jump.

Fig.77 (top). This figure shows the starting position for the squat-thrust exercise. In essence, it is the same position as for the start of the press up exercise. Although a strength-endurance exercise predominantly for the legs, there is also an effect on the arms and abdominals.

Fig.78. (above) Once the squat-thrust exercise begins both legs are thrust forward as quickly as possible into the position shown. The legs are then thrust back equally quickly into the start position as shown in the previous figure. This is the complete squat-thrust movement, which is repeated throughout the set time period.

appropriate height for the athletes. They then start with the bench at full extension from the wall bar against their chests. From here, they go down into a squat position and then drive upwards into the original position and, at the same time, lift the bench above their head with the arms fully extended. They then continue to repeat the exercise (Fig. 79).

Stage Training

Stage training is an extension of circuit training where the emphasis is on specific exercises and the time spent on each activity. In a normal circuit the athlete would rotate from exercise to exercise for three circuits. Therefore, after completing a leg exercise (step-ups), he would move to an exercise on his arms (dips), then to an abdominal exercise (inclined sit-ups) and then to a general exercise (burpees). However, with stage training the athlete would remain at the same exercise for all three circuits, three leg exercises, before moving to the next three exercises on his arms. In this way there is a great increase of local muscular fatigue in a specific part of the body, such as the legs, whereas with a general circuit this build up will not be as acute. This is because he will move next to an arm exercise, then to an abdominal exercise and then to a general exercise and the local muscular fatigue in the legs will have been dispersed by the time of the next leg exercise (*see* Fig. 80).

Fig.79. Bench raises are a general endurance exercise which may be made specific to just the arms if the full exercise is not completed. The exercise begins with the athlete in a semi-squat position with the bench against the athlete's chest. He then drives upwards from the feet into a standing position; the bench is then pushed upwards with the arms at full extension and the feet also drive upwards onto the toes. He then returns to the original position and continues to repeat the exercise.

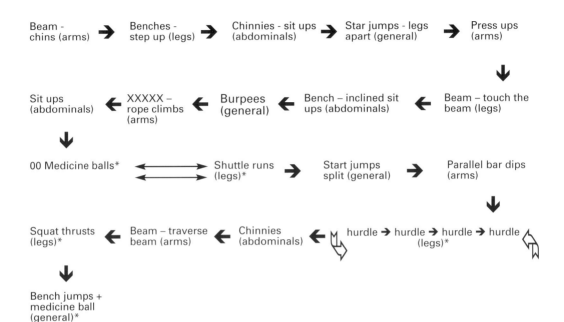

Beam - chins (arms) → Benches - step up (legs) → Chinnies - sit ups (abdominals) → Star jumps - legs apart (general) → Press ups (arms) ↓

Sit ups (abdominals) ← XXXXX – rope climbs (arms) ← Burpees (general) ← Bench – inclined sit ups (abdominals) ← Beam – touch the beam (legs) ↓

00 Medicine balls* ↔ Shuttle runs (legs)* → Start jumps split (general) → Parallel bar dips (arms) ↓

Squat thrusts (legs)* ← Beam – traverse beam (arms) ← Chinnies (abdominals) ← hurdle → hurdle → hurdle → hurdle (legs)* ↓

Bench jumps + medicine ball (general)*

*centre of gymnasium

Fig.80. This general circuit is using gymnastic apparatus and is designed to build up strength-endurance (local muscular endurance). The activities rotate from an arm exercise, to a leg exercise, to an abdominal exercise and then a general exercise and from then on the process is repeated with different exercises. This type of circuit may also be used for stage training. The number of sets and the duration of each exercise is determined by the athlete's ability and fitness level.

Also included is a circuit requiring no gymnastic apparatus, which can be done at home in the carport, in the living room or at the track. This circuit is convenient and saves time in travelling to a gymnasium or fitness centre. It can easily be adapted to stage training as the athlete gets fitter. Similarly, as he enters the specific preparation phase the circuit can be altered and made even more so to his individual needs as long as there is no gymnastic equipment required.

The exercises involved in the non-apparatus circuit are:

• press ups (arms);
• squat thrusts (legs) (as in Fig. 77 and 78);
• chinnies (abdominal) (as in Fig.72);
• star jumps with the legs split (general) (as in Fig.75 and 76);
• triceps dips (arms) (see Fig. 81 and 82);
• donkey kicks: squat thrusts with legs alternating (legs) (see Fig. 83);
• inclined sit ups (abdominal);
• burpees (general);
• inclined press-ups (arms) (see Fig. 84);
• high knees (legs) (see Fig. 85);
• half sit-ups (abdominal);
• star jumps with the legs together (general) (as in Fig.73).

The circuit of twelve exercises should build up to a maximum of three circuits with 1min on each exercise, a 30sec recovery and 1min 30sec between sets.

Fig.83. Donkey kicks (Oregon circuit) are a similar exercise to squat thrusts (see Fig.77 and 78). However, instead of having the legs operating together as in squat thrusts, they are split as in the photograph. With the arms stationary, the legs repeatedly change positions as quickly as possible for the duration of the exercise.

Fig.81. Triceps dips can be performed by using a park bench, a chair, a doorstep or anything else that can be suitably improvised. Both the arms and the legs are at full extension with the body upright and the hands gripping the bench.

Fig.84. Using any suitable raised, but not too tall object, the legs are placed together on it with the arms extended in front. To execute the inclined press-up, the arms are lowered to a 90 or other suitable angle, as shown in the photograph, held and then the arms are fully extended back to the original position. This is repeated.

Fig.82. The arms are lowered, still keeping the body upright and the legs extended, until the elbows are at 90 degrees. The position is held and then the arms are extended again until they return to the position in Fig.81. This is then repeated continuously. This exercise is good for strengthening the arms, particularly the triceps and the abdominal area.

The Oregon Circuit

This was devised at Oregon University specifically for middle-distance runners, and was popularized by Joaquim Cruz, the Olympic 800m champion. With this type of circuit the exercises are predominantly for the legs as are all the recoveries. Unlike the normal indoor circuit training, between both exercises and circuits all the recoveries are run at a brisk pace. This makes the circuit specific to middle-distance runners, improves the muscular endurance of the legs, but also the cardiovascular and the respiratory system. There are nine exercises involved: two for general mobility, two for general endurance and the other five are leg exercises. The exercises are as follows:

Fig.86. In the side swing exercise (Oregon circuit) the legs are shoulder-width apart, the arms stretched out at shoulder height with the head looking straight ahead. Still keeping the arms straight, the body is rotated as far to the left as possible with the eyes facing backwards. The body then returns to the front position and rotates as far as possible to the right. The exercise is repeated and each time the athlete tries to rotate a little further in each direction.

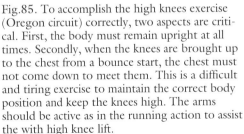

Fig.85. To accomplish the high knees exercise (Oregon circuit) correctly, two aspects are critical. First, the body must remain upright at all times. Secondly, when the knees are brought up to the chest from a bounce start, the chest must not come down to meet them. This is a difficult and tiring exercise to maintain the correct body position and keep the knees high. The arms should be active as in the running action to assist the with high knee lift.

- side swings (general mobility) (*see* Fig. 86);
- side stretches (general mobility) (*see* Fig. 87);
- burpees (general conditioning);
- star jumps (general conditioning) (as in Fig.75 and 76);
- high knees (legs) (*see* Fig. 85);
- shuttle run (legs) (*see* Fig. 89 on Oregon circuit for description);
- donkey kicks (legs) (*as in* Fig. 82);
- knees to chest (legs) – standing straight up, feet on the ground the athlete has to bring his knees up to his chest while remaining as straight as possible; he must not bend his back to meet his knees;
- leg claps (legs) (*see* Fig. 88).

Fig.87. The side stretch exercise (Oregon circuit) involves the athlete's standing with the legs shoulder-width apart, one arm curled up under the armpit, as in the photograph, the other arm extended down the side of the thigh. He then moves in this direction, extending the arm as far as possible down the leg then returns to the upright position. He then changes the position of his arms and repeats the exercise on the opposite side. He continues to change sides and repeat the exercise, keeping his back straight throughout. Photo: Spencer G. Duval

Strength-endurance can also be developed through running training; the main methods are:

• repetition work;
• hill or step work;
• turnabouts;
• back-to-back training;
• zigzag runs.

Fig.88. The picture shows the athlete demonstrating leg claps (Oregon circuit). She is bouncing as high as possible on one foot while the opposite leg is extended in front of her as near parallel to the ground as possible. The body must remain upright while the arms come together under the extended leg to perform the clap. The legs change position on the next bounce again, with a clap underneath the extended leg and then continue to repeat the exercise.

Three examples of strength-endurance repetition sessions are:

i. 10 × 400m in 60sec with a 45sec jogged recovery;
ii. 10 × 200m in 28sec with a constantly reduced recovery; the recovery would begin at 1min 30sec and fall after each recovery by 10sec until the final recovery period is only 10sec;
iii. 5 × (3 × 100m), 10sec hold between each repetitions and 1min 30sec between sets.

OREGON CIRCUIT.

- REST FOR 30 SECONDS AFTER EXERCISES 3 & 6
- STRIDE 100m BETWEEN EACH EXERCISE
- SHUTTLE RUN IS 10m/20m x 2
- AFTER EXERCISE 9 JOG A WHOLE LAP (1,000m) AND THEN REPEAT
- NUMBER OF EXERCISES AT EACH ACTIVITY AND NUMBER OF CIRCUITS DEPENDS ON THE ATHLETES AGE AND FITNESS.

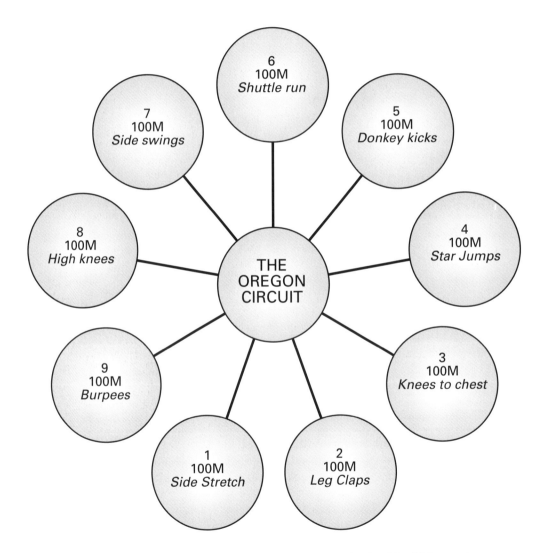

Fig.89. The Oregon circuit is conducted outdoors over a 1,000m circuit with a 100m run between each activity. At exercises three and six there is a 30sec recovery before the run. If a 1,000m circuit is not available a 100m football pitch may be used, with the recovery between each repetition being the length of the pitch and three whole laps of the pitch run for recovery between each circuit. The number of sets and the number of repetitions at each of the nine stages is dependent on the ability and fitness of the athlete.

Fig.90. Hill training may be used to improve either speed-endurance or strength-endurance. The distance covered, the gradient and the number of sets and repetitions will be determined by which of the two training systems is being used. The athlete in the picture is training for speed-endurance as he is using a small number of repetitions, a good recovery and is running over 100m. Whichever type of hill training is undertaken it is essential that good technique and relaxation should always be emphasized. Photo: Spencer G. Duval

Fig.91. Step training is exactly the same as hill training except that the steps in a stadium, in a multi-storey car park or whatever is readily available to replace the hill. The principle is exactly the same as that outlined in Fig. 90. Photo: Spencer G. Duval

Fig.92. This figure continues the sequence in step training, with the athlete powering up the steps with a vigorous arm drive, high front knee and driving off an extended rear leg. Photo: Spencer G. Duval

All three sessions, while looking reasonable on a training schedule, are very challenging and should be attempted only by the high-performance middle-distance runner.

Other running sessions to improve strength-endurance are hill running, step work, turnabouts, back-to-backs and zigzag runs. Hills can be tackled up an incline of 10 to 20 degrees, either on a road, in parkland, a forest, on grassland or a golf course. The distance, the number of sets and repetitions will vary depending on the event and the time of year. But once the runner is into the specific preparation phase the number of repetitions will be high and the distance of the repetition equivalent to the race distance. For example, a 1,500m runner would run over a distance totalling 1,500m.

This could comprise five repetitions of 300m. The recovery between repetitions would be a jog back recovery. Step running can be done in a stadium, at a multi-storey car-park or in an office building. It is a similar method to hill running but done in a more controlled environment. The principle of ensuring that the athlete has a high knee lift, drives off his rear leg and has active arms is the key to good technique and ensuring that the maximum benefit is derived from the hill or step sessions (*see* Fig. 90–2).

Turnabouts are similar to a shuttle run in which the athlete will run a large number of repetitions for a given time over a short distance and has to keep turning to run in the direction he has just come from. For example, he could run 12 × 60m, with a turn at each end, or run round a post. With a back-to-back session the athlete runs for a given distance, has a short rest and then repeats the distance again, the number of repetitions being small but with a reasonable number of sets. In a back-to-back session he might run 5 sets × (3 × 100m), with a 10sec recovery and 1min 30sec between sets, the total adding up to his race distance. Zigzag running (*see* Fig. 49) is over distances between 180 and 210m, but the athlete does not run in a straight line. The distance is split into 30m legs, each at 90 degrees to the last leg and marked by posts or cones. The athlete has therefore to repeatedly slow down, check his speed, turn and begin to work hard on the next leg. The recovery is a jogged recovery down the side of the course and the number of repetitions is high. This also simulates a race in which he will never have a clear run and is constantly checked and blocked by other athletes.

RESISTANCE TRAINING

This can either be used against the natural environment, such as mud, wind, snow, sand, surf, altitude or water, or it can be used against a force, such as towing, harness running, weighted belts, power suits and medicine ball work. It can be used with any training method from a steady-state run, hill work to repetition work, wherever the coach feels that it is applicable. The effect is an increase in muscular endurance and coordination. It applies to all endurance events, but particularly the middle-distance ones, and can be both general and specific, depending on the phase of the training year in which it is employed. Resistance training adds variety to the programme, it is a different challenge with good physiological benefits as well as psychological ones. It does not have to be used every week, but is beneficial during the preparation phase.

To use the natural environment as a resistance is both cheap and effective. Wind and mud are regularly available throughout the year, although snow is not now so frequent as it was in the past, but when it is it has the same conditioning effect. To use surf training and sand dune running – unless you are fortunately placed geographically – may require a certain amount of travelling. Simple things like running into the wind and over muddy terrain make the athlete much stronger and these are usually easy to find. The runner has to work much harder than in normal conditions and accentuate both his arm and his leg action much more. A mini-parachute may be purchased with an attached harness which can be fitted to the body. He can then run into the wind, catching the air in the parachute, which will act as extra resistance and force him to work against it. He must ensure, however, that he modifies his technique slightly, particularly when running on mud to compensate; this means a slight shortening of the stride and ensuring good foot placing.

Similarly, when running on sand dunes the athlete must ensure that he has a high knee lift to drive out of the sand, ensure that his landing foot is secure and that, as with running on mud, he does not slip backwards. Sand dune running may be incorporated with hill running. This is an excellent form of resistance training, ensuring good strength-endurance. Areas such as Methyr Mawr (South Wales) and Southport (Lancashire) may be recommended for this type of training. Likewise normal hill training, whether on grass, a road, in parkland or a forest, is a splendid form of resistance training, but it is particularly applicable to sand hill running, with the extra underfoot resistance added to the resistance of the hill itself. Running in surf, up to mid-calf in height, is not only good conditioning work but also both invigorating and therapeutic for the legs.

Altitude training should be used carefully and at specific times of the year. To obtain the best effects the length of the stay at altitude should be for a minimum of two to three weeks, repeated often throughout the year and at a height of between 1,800 to 2,200m. The initial training should be of low intensity until the body has become acclimatized to this different environment. The more frequent the visits to altitude, the quicker the acclimatization. The effect of going to altitude is that it builds up the erythrocyte volume (red blood cells) so that oxygen utilization is improved, as is the tolerance to lactic acid. It is particularly effective during the competition period and will achieve the best effects from 21 to 28 days after returning. Altitude training effects can persist for up to six weeks after the athlete returns to sea level, or until the blood cells created at altitude die and are not replaced because the altitude effect is no longer present. After an initial uplift in performance upon returning to sea level, there will be a dip before the athlete returns to high performance levels. Precautions should be taken at altitude with regard to sleep hydration and exposure to the sun. If the runner is unable, because of time commitments, to go away to higher areas, an altitude tent may be purchased to simulate it for both training (on a treadmill in the tent) and sleeping in overnight.

Water training in a swimming pool, either with or without a wet-vest, is highly beneficial. It is useful when the athlete is injured, but is also good for building and maintaining the oxygen base, and, because there is no weight bearing, there is no stress on the legs. With water training the athlete will replicate either an aerobic run, and spend the same duration in the water, or a repetition session. The same technique as in running should be employed, with a vigorous arm and leg action to keep the torso as high above the water as possible. If he is not a good swimmer nor very buoyant a wet-vest or buoyancy aid can be used (*see* Fig. 101–103).

Harness running and towing exercises have to be used judiciously and correctly so that there is no injury to the athlete and no risk of impairing his technique. With both these methods the harness or the weight being towed can be either fixed to a static object or pulled by the athlete. Examples suitable for these exercises are harnesses, tyres, wall bars, parachutes or rollers. The emphasis at all times is on correct technique and the driving phase of running.

When a belt around the waist containing weights is used the athlete can do any of his normal training but accompanied by the belt. This could include steady-state training repetition work, hill training or circuit training. The coach will decide the weight to be placed in the belt, which can be increased or decreased depending on the time of the year and the desired training effect. These particular training methods are good for strengthening the abdominal and the lower back muscles. But because training with an additional weight may affect his centre of gravity and his technique, he must ensure that he is totally concentrated on running correctly at all times in training. Once the weighted belt is removed, not only is the athlete stronger but also more powerful

Fig.93. A resistance training aid is the power suit, which is used when running. The suit fits tightly to the skin and has Velcro pockets placed at strategic muscle areas around the body. Weights of varying size in the shape of tablets can then be placed into all or only particular pockets. This figure shows a frontal picture with weights attached to the shoulders, wrists and thighs (quadriceps). Photo: Spencer G. Duval

because he is free from the additional weight.

Similarly with hill training to improve his arm strength and arm drive, he can carry small dumb-bells or pebbles in his hands to increase the muscular endurance in his arms. A power suit (*see* illustration), unlike the two previous methods which are working on specific areas of the body which require strengthening, may be either specific or be a total body strength training programme. The athlete wears a suit similar to a leotard

Fig.94. This side view of the power suit shows further attachments to the calves (gastrocnemius) and the rear upper back. There are also pockets on the bottom (gluteus). The suit can be used with all duration training methods and hill or step training. Photo: Spencer G. Duval

Fig.95. A type of resistance training which can be used occasionally to add variety to training is the army-style assault course. This is good for strength-endurance (local muscular endurance) development for all areas of the body. This figure shows the athlete attacking the rope climb halfway round the course. Photo: Spencer G. Duval

containing pockets around the major muscle group areas where weights can be inserted. Like the weighted belt, the weight inserted will be determined by his fitness, the time of year and the effect required. Most training methods utilizing the power suit can be undertaken. However, this suit can become quite hot and the training sessions undertaken with it should not be too long since wearing it is demanding and tiring (*see* Fig. 93 and 94).

Another type of resistance training to be used occasionally to introduce variety is the army type of assault course (Fig. 95). This is a first-rate method of testing muscular endurance over a timed course. This will include a variety of obstacles which will test the strength-endurance of the arms, the legs and the abdominal area, as well as the general total strength and condition of the athlete. It can also give him a psychological boost if he performs well, in what is a non-threatening, competitive environment.

The aim of all these types of resistance training, as well as bringing in variety, is to make him work harder against a given resistance or force. This may be the environment, a weight or a manufactured resistance such as a harness. All conditioning work should be introduced during the general preparation phase and the greatest intensity of conditioning work will be during the specific preparation phase.

It is important that conditioning or strengthening training is continued throughout the whole season. This will not entail as many strength or conditioning sessions as during the specific preparation phase, nor will there be as many exercises or repetitions involved. The core idea of this type of training is 'to use it or lose it'. Far too many athletes and coaches stop all strength and conditioning work as they enter the pre-competitive phase: what this means is that all the conditioning and strength work they have done since October and the accumulative effects they have gained will be lost by stopping in May and the whole effect by the time of the competitive phase in late July and August. This type of training must be continued in a reduced form to maintain the effects gained during the general and the specific preparation phase, and to take them through into the pre-competition and the competition phase.

CHAPTER 5

Injury Prevention

No athlete likes to be inactive and therefore, to ensure that all the planning and preparation reach fruition, athlete and coach should be proactive and not reactive in ensuring that any missed training due to injury or illness is kept at a minimum. There are two key approaches which should be adopted if this is to succeed. The first is to ensure that the training is not only correctly balanced but is not all done on the same surface and includes non-weight bearing training, rest and regeneration. The second is having in place the correct support systems, which are not only instantly available if there is a problem but are used to avoid any problems or minor ones becoming major.

AVOIDANCE

There are a variety of ways to ensure that athletes are not subjected continually to road training and the pounding on the legs that this entails. The first is to ensure, particularly if the athlete is covering large distances, that a high proportion of training is done off-road (*see* Fig. 96 and 97), on far more forgiving surfaces than roads provide. Constant training on hard road surfaces or synthetic tracks can lead to injuries such as 'shin splints' or 'stress fractures'. Alternative surfaces that may be used include grassland, forest paths, parkland, playing fields, sand, surf and golf courses; what all these have in common is the fact that they are much easier

Fig.96. This figure shows an excellent example of 'off-road' running on forest paths with soft underfoot terrain which is forgiving to the legs. This type of environment can be used for every method of endurance duration training. Photo: Spencer G. Duval

on the legs and therefore provide less chance of injury. They also bring variety and a change of environment to the training programme. By watching the number of

Fig.97. Another type of 'off-road' training environment is grass, which is also sympathetic to the legs. This type of training environment is available to virtually everyone. Photo: Spencer G. Duval

Fig.98. Cross-country ski machines provide an ideal way of retaining aerobic fitness and ensuring that there are other than only impact sessions in training. These machines can be found at fitness centres or purchased for home use, as shown in the picture. This shows the legs in action, with the arms maintaining the body's balance. Photo: Spencer G. Duval

miles run by his athlete and ensuring that there are a variety of terrain types for him to train on, the coach is being proactive in ensuring that his athlete is less likely to pick up an injury.

There are other methods a coach can include in the training routine to ensure that his athletes are not injured; these are sometimes referred to as 'cross-training' because they ensure that he maintains his aerobic base and cardiovascular fitness while having no weight bearing on his legs. With this type of training he can do all of the aerobic training methods covered in Chapter 3. The two main non-weight-bearing exercises are water training and cycling. In both much aerobic training can be done with no impact loading stress being put on the legs. The cycling can be done on a racing, a mountain or a static cycle. Water training, in particular, may also be used if an athlete has, in fact, suffered injury and needs to keep up his aerobic fitness base, avoid customary training surfaces and avoid using his injured leg.

Another type of cross-training involves the cross-country ski-machine, where the legs move in a skiing motion on a static machine; because it is so smooth the machine avoids any jarring or impact problems (*see* Fig. 98–100). Once the technique has been mastered, heavy sessions can be undertaken, but, because of the technique, it is difficult to do high-intensity sessions on this machine. These machines can now be found in many fitness centres. This type of training is very good for maintaining a good aerobic level since cross-country skiers have some of the highest maximum VO2 readings in the world. However, cross-country ski training is not a substitute for running training because the action required for it differs from that used in the normal running action. It is also best, particularly with an injured athlete to use it in conjunction with water training or cycling to get the higher intensity sessions into the training programme. It is also possible to use the machine to strengthen the upper body

Fig.99. In this picture of the cross-country ski machine the legs are again active and have changed position. The arms are being used only as a counterbalance. However, the more accomplished the athlete becomes on these machines the more he can increase the tension on the arms so that they are working against a resistance and therefore gaining in strength. Photo: Spencer G. Duval

Fig.100. This close-up of the legs in action on the cross-country ski machine show the action of the right leg, with the heel raised and the right ski moving backward. The technique is dissimilar to a normal running action and therefore it is advisable to use this method judiciously. However, cross-country skiers have the highest maximum volume uptakes in the world and therefore this is a beneficial method of maintaining aerobic fitness. Photo: Spencer G. Duval

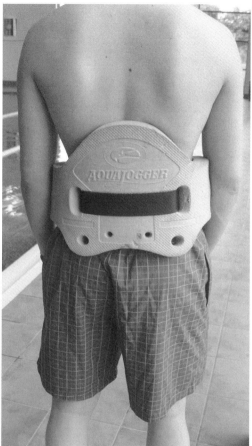

Fig.101. Aerobic training can be maintained using water training. This can be used for normal endurance training methods to take pressure off the legs or when the athlete is injured. This figure shows a wet-vest which will help to keep the athlete buoyant when in the water to ensure that the correct techniques can be practised. Photo: Spencer G. Duval

against different resistances to improve conditioning at the same time and used in conjunction with a heart-rate monitor it is an ideal way of maintaining aerobic fitness.

Running in water is nearer to the actual technique of running. If possible, it is preferable to train in water without a buoyancy aid or wet vest. However, if an athlete is not a good swimmer it would be advisable for him to use one. The technique

Fig.102. A side view of water training: the normal running action is used and the feet are off the bottom of the pool. It is important to keep the upper body as high above the water as possible and to try to use a normal running action. Photo: Spencer G. Duval

Fig.103. This figure shows a rear view of water training. The leg action is normal and active but the arm action here is not a normal running action but is being used more to keep the athlete afloat and upright in the water. Athletes who are not natural swimmers may need to use this technique initially to gain confidence. Photo: Spencer G. Duval

is to keep as high as possible in the water, using the arms as a driving force and the knees in a high driving position; it resembles running on the spot (*see* Fig. 102–103). In this way the runner can either work for a given time, such as 45min, to simulate an aerobic run, or repetition sessions of 6 × 3min, with 1min recovery, all this work taking place in the pool, including recovery. As an alternative, the athlete could swim a large number of lengths to build up his aerobic base and give his legs a rest from a constant pounding on the roads. Heart-rate monitors can be used in these water sessions so that comparative readings can be made with normal training loads to ensure that work rates are at the correct level.

With cycling any one of the types of machine listed above may be used: the static model, found in most leisure centres, or a conventional cycle to use on the road or a mountain cycle for rougher terrain. Once again, a large number of miles can be achieved without much stress on the legs and a high aerobic level can be achieved and maintained. With cycling, the training session may be either for a set time or a set distance. With a normal cycle training session the different types of terrain will provide the resistance required to make him work harder. When using a static cycle the resistance is provided by the controls on the machine.

A correct warm-up is essential if injury is to be prevented. It is of the utmost importance that the body is thoroughly warmed up and mobile before the start of the training session, particularly if it is a high-intensity session. The warm-up should include jogging, stretching or dynamic stretching, strides and acceleration runs (*see* Fig. 105) to ensure that the athlete is thoroughly prepared without the risk of injury which could be caused by an inadequate warm-up.

Fig.105. This shows two athletes completing a series of strides before starting a repetition endurance-training session on grass. Strides should be used in most warm-up sessions but particularly before high-intensity sessions. They may be performed on grass, golf courses, an indoor track, a sports hall or a synthetic surface. The strides should be over 50 to 80m and can be either at one constant speed or an ever-increasing speed. The aim is to have the body correctly prepared for the main part of the training session.

Fig.104. Cycle training is another excellent example of retaining aerobic fitness while ensuring that the legs are not being constantly exposed to impact training. This figure shows the athlete using a static cycle, but a normal racing cycle or mountain cycle is just as effective. Again, the normal duration training methods can be used on any of the cycles. Photo: Spencer G. Duval

REST AND REGENERATION

This is a key area in aiding recovery and one often neglected by athletes. Too many continue to train hard when a rest day would be far more beneficial and productive. Increased training loads require an increased recovery to ensure the appropriate adaptation. This is particularly important after high-intensity training sessions (*see* Fig. 106). Failure to restore it to its normal state results in overtraining and the incorrect training effect.

After a high-intensity training session there will be an increase in the pulse rate, body temperature and muscle soreness as well as an accumulation of metabolic by-products. There will also be a decrease in fluids, energy reserves and a reduction in the immune system. Therefore the sooner the body is returned to homeostasis the better. It is important therefore that immediately after such a session lost fluids are replaced and that a low-intensity, cool-down period of jogging and stretching takes place (*see* Fig. 107). This will help the utilization of lactate and its removal along with waste products from muscle tissues. It will assist the gradual return to normal of both the body's core temperature and the pulse rate and help to prevent blood pools from occurring at the body's extremities. In addition, it will lower both the hormonal levels and the psychological level of arousal, which were brought about by the training. It will further assist in the removal of muscle spasms and the effects of muscle soreness.

Loading	Running time (RT)	Recovery time	Recovery activity
Short Speed (all out)	10sec	3 x RT	Walking and/or stretching
(anaerobic capacity training)	20sec	3 x RT	Jogging
	30sec		
Long speed (95–100% of maximal effort) (anaerobic capacity training	30sec	3 x RT	Jogging
	60sec	2 x RT	Jogging
	80sec		
Speed + endurance (90–95% of maximal effort) (VO₂max to aerobic capacity training)	80sec	3 x RT	Jogging
	2min 40sec	1 x RT	Rest
	3min		
Endurance (80–90% of maximal effort) (anaerobic conditioning)	3min	1 x RT	Rest
	4min	0.5 x RT	Rest
	20min		

Fig.106. After high-intensity training sessions it is always wise to replenish the body with both liquid, preferably isotonic, and food, preferably carbohydrates. This is not only to feed the body but to help the immune system to recover. The following session should be of low intensity to help the body to adapt to the previous training load. This figure shows the recommended recovery times required during specific sessions to ensure that the athlete does not overtrain.

Rest is a specific training unit which allows the body to recover, recharge and replenish ready for the next training unit. It can be either passive rest, where no physical activity takes place with plenty of relaxation and sleep, or active rest, where another physical activity such as orienteering, swimming or cycling can be undertaken. It is important therefore that it is included in the training programme to aid the recovery phase.

Regeneration is an additional aid in accelerating the body's recovery so that it returns to normality as quickly as possible. It can be dealt with in a variety of ways, from simple rehydration, to massage, sauna, ice therapy, hydrotherapy or a cold bath.

With rehydration the aim is to replace the depleted energy reserves, fluid electrolytes and carbohydrates as quickly as possible.

Fig.107. After a high-intensity training session it is advisable to follow it through with a very low-intensity cool down. The figure shows athletes of all ages having an enjoyable, easy cool down. Sometimes it is advisable to send the high performer on a cool down with slower athletes to ensure that their cool down is of the low intensity required. Photo: Spencer G. Duval

Massage increases the muscle blood flow, stimulates the nervous system, reduces muscle tightness and anxiety levels, and gives the athlete a feeling of well-being. For these reasons, and for any early warning signs of injury, massage is highly beneficial in quickly restoring an athlete to normal and has both a physical and a psychological effect on him.

Massage should be undertaken as often as possible depending on your finances, and particularly after high-intensity training sessions. The use of a sauna should be followed by a cold plunge; this is because the heat from the sauna has stimulated the blood to help in reducing the waste products in the system, muscle soreness and tightness, and then the body is reinvigorated by a cold plunge. Ice therapy or an ice massage reduces the fluid build-up in the muscles and post-exercise soreness. Cold baths, where the legs and other parts of the body are wholly or partially immersed for up to a minute (depending on how used to this method the athlete is), have a similar effect. Hydrotherapy involves the use of either hot and cold showers or hot and cold spas or baths, and is comparable to other regeneration methods. The shower method, which may be used at any time of the day, should comprise a warm or hot shower for 1 to 2min and then a cold shower for 10 to 30sec (again, depending on how used to this method the athlete is); this process should be repeated three times. With the spa or bath method the athlete should stay in the warm or hot spa or bath for 3 to 4min and in the cold one for 30 to 60sec; this too should be repeated three times. This is best used at the end of the day, but not, however, if the athlete has a cold or other infection or has had a recent soft tissue injury.

All of these methods of rest, whether active or passive, and regeneration are vitally important in helping the athlete's body to return to normal as quickly as possible, avoid injury and be ready for the next training session. For preference, these therapies should be built into the training programme as specific sessions. It is crucially important that the programme does not cause the athlete to overtrain, strain, plateau or become stale. The coach must constantly monitor his athlete to ensure that none of these occurs.

TRAINING VS. STRAINING

One of the real tests of a good coach is what he does when things are not going well with his athlete. This may be due to injury, in which case there are specialists in certain areas, such as doctors, physiotherapists, masseurs, osteopaths and surgeons, whom the coach can call upon to find both the cause and the remedy for the problem. It is, however, when the athlete loses form that the mettle of the coach is really tested.

In many cases some coaches see the answer as doing more training, whether this is more mileage, more repetitions, more intense sessions or even more sessions. This is usually the last thing that the athlete needs, sometimes more means less in terms of performance. In any good coach–athlete relationship a frank, open discussion will pinpoint the problem(s) if the observant coach has not done so already.

A good coach, above all, is constantly evaluating his athlete's progress, increasing both the load and the intensity progressively. He must be aware of the athlete's strengths and weaknesses and ensure that the balance of training meets the requirements of the event his athlete has chosen. The coach must set realistic targets, motivate and support him and ensure that the agreed training programme is implemented correctly.

If all these criteria are adhered to it should help the coach, when the athlete loses form, to eliminate certain factors quickly and to determine why the athlete has lost form or gone stale. It could be one simple reason or a combination of them, since many external factors can influence both the athlete's performance and his attitude. The following checklist is a guideline to some of the reasons which may account for a loss of form and the possible solutions to it. It is to help the coach to monitor his athlete and ensure that he is not overtraining nor straining.

TRAINING VS. STRAINING CHECKLIST

Work Stresses

Cause: long hours, physically demanding work, shift work, examinations.
Solution: training must be tailored to the athlete's demands; easy sessions should be placed on his demanding work days, double sessions or intense sessions on his less demanding days; the rest and regeneration sessions are invaluable to the athlete in this situation.

Emotional Stresses

Cause: family, work, relationships, money and friends.
Solution: have a constant dialogue with your athlete; in this way you can head off any problems or be in a far better position either to solve the problem or be supportive, this helps to take the pressure off the athlete and gives him a stable base.

Social Stresses

Cause: peer pressure, religious beliefs, conflict of interests, life style.
Solution: encourage the athlete and make him feel valued; re-emphasize his goals in view of the current situation.

Dietary Stresses

Cause: incorrect eating, at an inappropriate time, incorrect type of food, junk food, not enough food, insufficient vitamins and supplements.
Solution: check the athlete's weekly food intake on a regular basis, suggest a good healthy balanced diet which will cover the requirements needed to meet the training programme and ensure that he is taking the correct supplements and vitamins.

Training Too Intensively

Cause: too much mileage, too many sessions, sessions too intense, no variety in the training, incorrect energy pathways being covered, balance of training inappropriate, poor use of rest and regeneration, over-racing.
Solution: one or a combination of the following suggestions should help the situation: reduce the mileage and the number of training sessions, lower the intensity and include more rest and regeneration in the training; add variety; re-evaluate the training and the racing programme for the time of year, the event and the athlete, particularly in regard to some of these suggestions; never follow one high-intensity session by another; do not leave all the good work in training, taper for the competition to produce the best.

Health Stresses

Cause: training too hard can exacerbate simple health problems and minor injuries; coupled to eating incorrectly and any other stresses, it may lead to the athlete's breaking down.
Solution: the athlete should not train too hard if he is carrying any infection, take a few days rest, have regular blood checks for conditions such as anaemia, periodically check diet for any signs of incorrect eating.

Environmental Stresses

Cause: city life, travel, home or lodgings, work, facilities, pollution.
Solution: tailor the training to meet the demands of the environment, help him to plan and organize his life style.

Psychological Pressures

Cause: expectations too high from self, family, friends, club, media, governing body.

Solution: make the goals realistic and attainable, reassess them constantly, be positive, ensure that the athlete goes into the most important race in the best condition both physically and mentally.

Finance

Cause: lack of financial support could hinder optimal performance and the athlete could become vulnerable to the previously mentioned stresses.
Solution: try to get a good support system in place for the athlete to use when required, and actively seek sponsorship.

School, College, University and Club Pressures

Cause: conflict with institutions demanding athlete's time can cause a crisis of conscience and lead to an unsettled state.
Solution: athlete's aims take precedence, ensure that the goals for the season are taken into account; institutions are only a competition vehicle for the athlete.

Feeling Undervalued

Cause: by club, coach, group, school, college, university or community.
Solution: build up the athlete's self-esteem; be positive at all times; no one competes badly on purpose.

Time Management

Cause: lack of the constructive and quality use of the time that is available.
Solution: sit down with the athlete and help him to plan his time; maximise the free time he has available for training, resting and socializing.

There are undoubtedly more causes to add to the list, however, this should give the coach a greater insight into some of the reasons why an athlete may lose form or go stale. A good coach has an eye that will recognize these symptoms and he should thereby be able to pinpoint the reasons for any loss of form. He should then be able to eradicate them swiftly.

An optimally trained athlete as defined by POMS (Profile of Mood States, J. Kimiecik [1988]) is *low* in tension, depression, anger, anxiety, confusion, and fatigue, but *high* on vigour and vitality. Whereas an overtrained athlete shows a reversal of these conditions.

SUPPORT SYSTEMS

The coach and the athlete should be constantly monitoring for any injuries caused by overuse. Because the legs and the feet take most of the impact in training, these are where most injuries will occur. The most common, apart from muscle pulls, strains or tears are the following:-

- periostitis (shin splints)
- tendonitis (mainly at the insertion of the tendon)
- knee problems (either to the outer ligaments or wearing at the knee joint [patella tendon syndrome])
- foot injuries (mainly to the fore and middle foot)
- Achilles tendon problems.

The athlete therefore should always be proactive by ensuring that he uses dynamic exercise in his warm-up, and static exercises at the end of the session to get rid of any stiffness and soreness. Daily mobility exercises in the evening are also a good way of preventing minor injuries which could become major. The occasional aerobic training session in the swimming pool, on a cross-country ski machine or bicycle to reduce weight bearing, described earlier, also has its advantages. Similarly, off-road running is an excellent way of avoiding injury. However, to ensure that his athlete

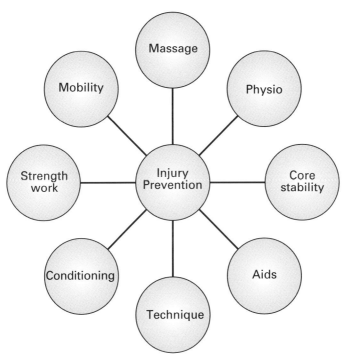

Fig.108. Along with the correct diet, hydration and cool down, this figure shows other methods which will help injury prevention and stop illness, from massage through to aids such as vitamins and supplements. These should all be part of the training programme and work in tandem with the support systems that are in place.

is constantly monitored and any minor complaint, strain or impending injury is nipped in the bud, the coach should have in place a network of support systems (*see* Fig. 31). This is being both proactive and, in certain cases, reactive. The objective is to ensure that the athlete does not get injured, but, if he does, to keep his missed training to a minimum. In this way he will be back running as quickly as possible.

These support systems are to ensure that the early signs of injury are acted upon quickly and immediately, and, if an athlete is injured, that the support systems are there to prevent the injury becoming more serious. The support systems should include a masseur, physiotherapist, doctor, sports scientist, bio-mechanic, podiatrist, sponsorship, nutritionist, psychologist and conditioner if required (*see* Fig.108).

Massage

To ensure that the legs are well maintained, the athlete and the coach can use self-massage. This is not only immediate but saves time and is obviously cost-effective, particularly for the athlete who has little or no sponsorship. This self-massage is best done after training but it can also be used last thing at night or first thing in the morning, particularly if there is tightness, stiffness or soreness. If a particular condition persists it is advisable to go to a professional masseur (*see* Fig. 109–113).

It is always advisable, if the finances allow, to have a massage at least once a week, particularly after any intense training sessions. In this way the masseur will eradicate any tightness, stiffness or soreness in the muscles and get rid of any waste

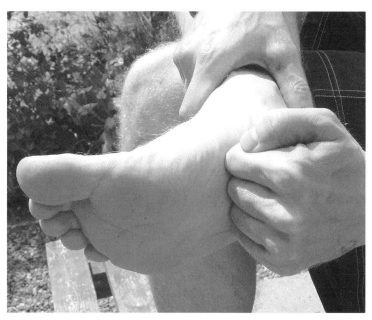

Fig.109. Feet absorb shock as the runner pounds along during a competition or training routine. However, unless they become blistered they tend to be neglected. It is quite easy to massage the feet in a sitting position with one leg crossed over the other, freeing both hands. Using the thumbs or fingers, small circular movements should be made across the sole of the foot, including the heel pad and the base of the toes. Then repeat using a clenched fist along the sole and the arch. This should be done on both feet to get rid of any stresses or strains and in conjunction with massaging the toes. Photo: Spencer G. Duval

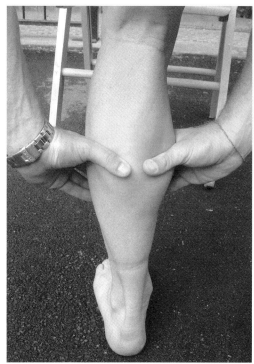

Fig.110. The two major muscles of the calf are the gastrocnemius and soleus muscles. They join at the heel through the Achilles tendon, an extremely strong tendon, which is susceptible to injury. The other minor muscles are important for balance and regulating the runner's gait. The tendons from the two major calf muscles are attached at the knee. It is important therefore that this particular area, which has so much stress placed on it, is well maintained.

The aim of self-massage is to repair these hard worked muscles, which can become stiff or sore through intense training or running on a hard or uneven surface. In this figure, drawing the thumbs across the muscle towards the fingers and moving up each leg is pressing on the calf muscle. This is then repeated, drawing the fingers to the thumbs across the fibres in the other direction. The fingers of each hand can also be gently drawn together up the centre of the calf dividing the muscle bulk in two. The aim is to reduce any swelling, remove any damaged cells and open the channels again for normal movement. Photo: Spencer G. Duval

products. The massage assists circulation, reduces pain, disperses scar tissue and adhesions and realigns muscle fibres, all of which speed up recovery. It also helps with the stretching of the muscles and the tendons of the body and leaves the athlete with a feeling of well-being. It could also help in diagnosing the early signs of any

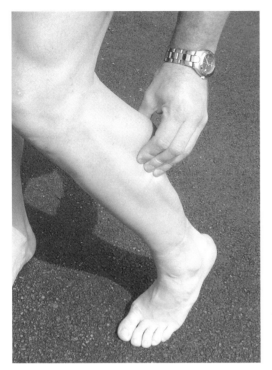

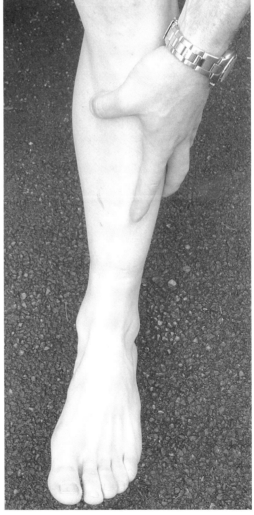

Fig.111. (left) In this exercise the calf muscle is being squeezed. Taking hold of handfuls of muscle, press the thumb and fingers into them and then let go. Work from the bottom of the leg to the top, squeezing with alternate hands and then let go and repeat on the other leg. Once a comfortable method has been found this is very beneficial. Both sections should be done twice, with an emphasis on pressing in towards the bone on the second occasion. It is also advisable to use the flushing motion to warm up the muscle before starting any self-massage exercises. Flushing is stroking with one flat hand after another, all around the leg for 30sec on each leg. Flushing and friction are useful when used in the Achilles area. Photo: Spencer G. Duval

Fig.112. (right) The shin is an important and often injured area. This is because there is only one major muscle (tibialis) placed under a great deal of stress. This area also has a low blood supply and injuries are therefore more painful than elsewhere. The massage in this area should be gentle and avoid any lumps or bruised areas. Flushing strokes towards the body should be used, with one hand following the other. Friction movements in little circles, using the thumbs will reduce any swelling after a bruise. To avoid or help with shin splints, a painful injury that runs up the side of the shin, the flushing and circular movements should be used with the pad of the thumb. It takes several days to pass and the pain is quite severe. The knuckles may also be used on certain areas of the lower leg to get deeper, once the muscle has been thoroughly warmed up. Other types of massage which are useful before a race are shaking, which involves taking hold of the centre portion of the muscle in the hand and shaking it; how hard it is done depends on the athlete, and it should be done in different areas; and finally tapping, which involves using alternate loose fists to tap all along the muscles from the ankle to the knee. These two exercises are to liven up the muscles before a race and are not suitable for use after competition or in training. Photo: Spencer G. Duval

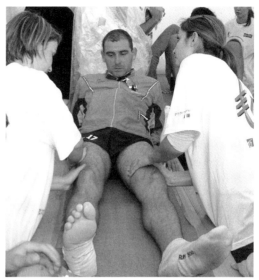

Fig.114. This figure shows physiotherapists working at the end of a race. In this situation any minor problem that may have occurred can be caught early before it becomes a major one. A high-performance athlete should have weekly contact with a physiotherapist, either at the track or at the physiotherapy clinic. Photo: Spencer G. Duval

Fig.113. The ankle is often a neglected area when it comes to a mobility routine. Because of the constant running done during a training programme, it tends to become stiff. Sitting on the floor or a seat with one leg crossed over the other, gently rotate the ankle clockwise for 30sec and then for the same period in an anti-clockwise direction. Then repeat for the other ankle. Photo: Spencer G. Duval

strain or impending injury and gives the observant athlete an opportunity to understand his body better. When allied to self-massage it could help in diagnosing any minor problems and in identifying a time to ease off in training. Massage is highly beneficial and invigorating, particularly when used in conjunction with the hydrotherapies.

Physiotherapy

A good physiotherapist is an integral part of the support team (see Fig. 114). If the funds will not allow for both a physiotherapist and a masseur it is better to involve the physiotherapist rather than the masseur and perform self-massage. In many cases lottery-funded athletes will get financial assistance with both physiotherapy and massage. Unlike a masseur, a physiotherapist can deal with any major strains, stresses, muscle tears or pulled muscles. He will not only be able to diagnose the problem but also cure it. With any major problem, such as an Achilles tendon injury, he will be able to advise on treatment or a possible operation.

Doctors and Drugs

A good relationship is required with a local doctor. He will not only be useful in taking blood samples to check haemoglobin levels and any signs of anaemia, but also to advise and monitor on any prescription drugs. This is particularly important for the high-performance athlete who is regularly drug-tested both in and out of the competition season. In conjunction with a physician, he can ensure that the runner is not taking any medicine which contains drugs on the banned list shown below. If an athlete qualifies for therapeutic use exemption (TUE) he will need supporting evidence from a doctor since this must be submitted to the competition's governing body. This is to ensure that he is covered if any effects of his prescription drugs show up in future testing, thus the use of asthma inhalers is covered by this category. If a good relationship is reached with a doctor, he could be of assistance if any major surgery were required, such as an Achilles tendon operation. The doctor has a large network of contacts, which could be accessed by the coach and his athlete.

IAAF-IOC Banned Drugs

The International Amateur Athletic Federation (IAAF) and the International Olympic Committee (IOC) have identified the following classes of banned drugs; for updates and the specifics of each category the coach and his athlete should refer to the relevant national governing body (United Kingdom Athletics, UKA, for British athletes).

Stimulants: to increase alertness, reactions and reduce fatigue (examples: amphetamines [in some tonics], ephedrine [in some cold cures])

Narcotic analgesics: to manage pain (examples: aspirin and codeine [found in cold remedies])

Anabolic steroids: to speed recovery, aid competitiveness, increase muscle bulk (examples: stanozolol, nandralone)

Beta blockers: to manage tension, help hand–eye coordination (examples: stenolol, proprandol, oxprendol [in medicines for hypertension])

Diuretics: to manage or lose body weight (examples: bumetanide, amiloride, benzthiazide)

Peptide hormones and analogues: human chorionic (similar to anabolic steroids) (example: pregnyl); corticotrophin: to increase blood levels of corticosteroids (example: synacthen); human growth hormones (HGH, to increase muscle hypertrophy and reduce ageing process) (example: humatrope, norditropin [medication to encourage growth]); erythropoetin (EPO, to increase erythrocyte volume/blood capacity).

Two important methods of doping are:
i. Pharmacological, chemical and physical manipulation.
   Precautions are in place to ensure that there is no tampering, nor altering of urine samples which would affect the validity of these samples during a controlled drug test.
   Examples of cheating include: urine substitution, use of a catheterization.
ii. Blood Doping
   To prevent this, blood transfusion can be taken from an endurance athlete, or another endurance athlete with the same blood group and then reinfused at a later date. The ideal time to take the transfusion is after altitude training. The blood is stored and usually reinfused before a major championship.

To remain constantly up to date with the list of currently prohibited drugs and discover whether or not an athlete qualifies for therapeutic use exemption, the coach and his athlete should use the available Internet sites. The three most useful ones are those of UKA (www.ukathletic.net), the IAAF (www.iaaf.org) and the World Anti-doping Agency (www.wada-ama.org).

Sports Scientists

Access to such specialists is also invaluable; a high-class performer on lottery funding will

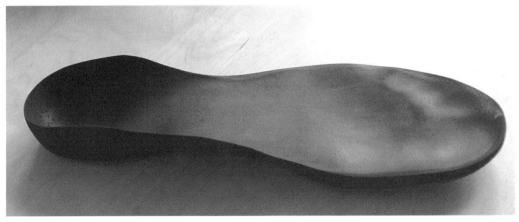

Fig.115. If there is any technical running problem this should have been picked up through having a biomechanical analysis. The problem will then be rectified by a podiatrist who will prepare inserts or orthotics built specifically for the individual athlete to address his problem. These may be quite costly and take a few weeks to be designed for the athlete. Photo: Spencer G. Duval

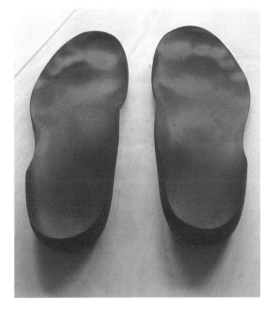

Fig.116. To ensure that the athlete's balance is maintained, two orthotics are made – one for each foot, which should be inserted into training shoes, racing shoes or spikes, whichever shoe he is wearing. These will then ensure that there is no overcompensation and that he remains correctly balanced. Photo: Spencer G. Duval

have this. However, if his athlete lacks this type of funding the coach should negotiate with the local university, which should have a sports science department, to ensure that his athlete is properly tested and monitored. The sort of help sport scientists can give includes blood testing and a range of other tests such as the measurement of fat levels, maximum VO2 and lactate. These tests should be done at regular intervals throughout the season to help in monitoring how training is progressing and to make any modifications or changes that may be necessary. The use of a sports scientist is invaluable in monitoring an athlete's training, maintaining the correct balance and ensuring that the correct progression is properly implemented. In this way, overtraining, staleness and stress can be either eradicated or spotted early enough for action to be successfully taken.

Biomechanics

The coach and his athlete should also ensure that they have the use of biomechanical analysis. In this way they can ensure that any problems in technique can be eradicated.

Many leg problems and injuries result from poor technique and are exacerbated by the distance he will do in training. If leg problems persist it could be because of poor technique. The coach should use the biomechanical information and enlist the help of a podiatrist. He will then be able to construct insoles, supports, inserts or orthotics (*see* Fig. 115–116) which will give his runner much greater stability, correct any problems and give greater protection to the legs from the constant wear and tear of training.

Finance

The coach must ensure that, if his athlete is not lottery-funded, he needs to look elsewhere for alternative methods of financial support. He should approach his athlete's club and employers to see whether they can give any support, using the argument that it will be good publicity for them when he is successful. He should approach the local and the county sports association as well as the local council; other possibilities include local businesses, national companies and the major manufacturers of kit and equipment. It may be that there is no specific financial support but some in terms of kit, time off work to train and help with transportation. The more financial support the athlete has, however, the easier it becomes to be a full-time athlete. He can then train and recover correctly without the demands of a job, either full-time or part-time. It will also allow him to access the support systems already mentioned.

Nutrition

It is useful to have access to a sports nutritionist so that the athlete's diet can be constantly monitored. Done over a period of time, this ensures that the correct fuel is being taken at the correct time and that the calorific intake is correct. It is particularly important that the correct nutrients, carbohydrates, fluids and proteins are taken, particularly after high-intensity training or competition. It is essential that the body tissues are repaired and that the body returns to homeostasis as quickly as possible. Therefore, if a three-weekly to monthly check is kept on his athlete's diet, the coach, in conjunction with the nutritionist, can ensure that there is no problem with the incorrect food and nutrients, junk food, hydration or calorific intake. The nutritionist can also recommend if vitamin or other supplements such as electrolyte drinks and creatine are required to supplement the diet. This is particularly important during intense training periods.

Psychologist

A psychologist may be required by only a few athletes who are either lacking in self-confidence or not producing the competition results that their training indicates. However, it could also be argued that all high-performance athletes should have access to a psychologist to be able to get even more out of themselves. A psychologist comes in as a fresh face and helps to build up an athlete's self-esteem; he may get the athlete to go through mental rehearsal exercises or look at the positive aspects of both his training and competitions; he may ask the athlete to think why a particular competition went well and get him to try and create a similar environment at his next competition. Whatever approaches the psychologist takes, together with the coach it is to try to get the athlete thinking and acting positively both in his training and particularly in his competitions – it may be the little impetus or edge that he requires to make the breakthrough and be successful.

Most coaches cannot be experts in all the areas relevant to their athletes' success. Therefore it may be necessary to enlist the help and support of other experts who can improve a particular area or requirement, it may mean enlisting the help of a strength conditioner to improve an athlete's general condition and strength-endurance, or a sprint coach to improve an athlete's basic speed and ability to accelerate, or another coach to check the basic technical model of his athlete to see whether he has any flaws or weaknesses, or a fitness instructor who will improve the suppleness and flexibility of the athlete. The coach should not be too proud to acknowledge the fact that he may not have enough expertise and experience in a certain field, and should therefore be willing to seek assistance from others.

Support systems, the correct balance to training, including rest and regeneration, have a dual role to play in an athlete's training programme. First, they are put in place to be proactive to ensure that the athlete does not get injured, ill nor overtrains. Secondly, they should already be in place to be reactive if injury, illness or overtraining does occur. In this way the problem can be nipped in the bud and dealt with quickly and effectively with the minimum of time lost away from training. Therefore it is crucial for the high-performance middle-distance runner that such support and injury-prevention systems are in place.

CHAPTER 6

Planning and Preparation

INTRODUCTION

When an athlete and his coach sit down at the end of a season to plan the athlete's training programme, the first thing they must do is to ensure that they evaluate the programme which has just been completed. From this they will be able to deduce where the athlete is at this stage in his development, what was successful in the previous season and what areas need work and further development. This evaluation is usually carried out during the transition phase, which occurs at the end of the track season when most athletes have a rest phase before they start the build-up for the following season. When doing this evaluation the coach and the athlete should use the following criteria and always remember that each athlete is an individual and should be so treated in all respects:

- the age of the athlete
- the number of years the athlete has been training
- the event and its requirements
- the athlete's strengths and weaknesses
- the training environment
- the previous season
- the aims – both short-term (season) and long-term (future).

Why do we need to evaluate? We need to assess where the athlete is at this point in his athletic development and to examine his strengths and weaknesses. We need to see what progress the athlete has made since the previous evaluation. It is also necessary to evaluate the athlete's yearly training programme. It commits the athlete's and the coach's views to paper and allows for both short- and long-term goals. It is also advisable for the athlete to keep his own daily training diary to which he can attach personal comments on his responses to the training, his state of health and personal commitments. He can also use it as part of the evaluation process with his coach. Finally, it can be used as a motivational tool.

What are the criteria for this evaluation process? They need to be objective so that the findings can be used in the next programme. They need to be reliable so that the evidence gathered is of benefit to the athlete and coach. They also need to be objective so that they take into consideration all aspects of the athlete's season. If he has missed a large part of the training through illness or injury this will obviously have an impact on his season and he will therefore have difficulty meeting the targets that have been set. The evaluation should measure more than one factor to give the whole picture; where possible they should involve technical input such as physiological testing procedures.

During this evaluation process the athlete and coach should use a planning review sheet (*see* below) and they should both come to the evaluation with their own views and input. The high-performance athlete will have more input than would a much younger, less experienced athlete. Using the information from the previous season's training programme, the athlete's progress can then be assessed. This assessment should include an examination of the athlete's strengths against the requirements for the event (*see* Fig. 5 on the qualities required for middle-distance events). It could be that at some stage the athlete and the coach decide that they have come as far as they possibly can in a particular event and need to look at another one more suited to the athlete's strengths. The factors set out below should be considered.

AGE

How old is the athlete? How much running or training background has he got? Is he physically mature for his age? How many times does he train a week? How interested or motivated is he?

ANATOMICAL CONSTRAINTS

When planning a programme for the younger athlete the constraints set out below are relevant factors. The ages cited in the table are approximate and based on chronological not biological ages; therefore consideration has to be taken of the early biological developer. The table emphasizes

	Girls	Boys
major height increases	11–12	14–15
major weight increases	11–12	13–14
optimum skill age 8–11	8–13	
heart volume (maximum)	11–13	13–20
maximum volume		
oxygen uptake 15–16	18–19	
maximum strength	16–17	18–19
glycogenic system		
(anaerobic work) 14	15	
(earliest) (earliest)		

how much more quickly females pass through adolescence and therefore reach their full development much earlier than males do.

STRENGTHS AND WEAKNESSES

The athlete's strengths and weaknesses must be pinpointed early and individual training programmes must allow for the strengths to be developed and the weaknesses to be eradicated. If, for example, an athlete has good endurance, this can be classified as a strength. However, if the athlete has poor mobility, this is classified as a weakness. The coach and the athlete should also, as shown on the planning sheet, be looking at the athlete's strengths and weaknesses in relationship to the qualities required for the chosen event.

THE EVENT

The event that the athlete is going to specialize in must be taken into account since this will affect the amount of loading, bias and the type of training included in the programme and its balance. The physiological requirements should also be used as one of the main criteria when assessing the athlete's strengths and weaknesses (*see* Fig. 4 on the physiological requirements for each event).

THE TRAINING ENVIRONMENT

The coach must know the advantages and disadvantages of his own training environment and must use these advantages to the full if his programme is to have variety and be successful. He must also ensure that the advantages neutralize the disadvantages. The coach must make the environment work for the athlete and, in choosing where and when the training sessions take place, he must take into account the athlete's home circumstances, his working day and the travel involved. He coach must also try to make the sessions varied, creative and, above all, enjoyable for the athlete.

SHORT-TERM AIM

Short-term aims usually involve planning for the forthcoming season. Therefore the finalizing of both a winter and a summer fixture list is an important part of this process. From these fixture lists the major events that you wish to concentrate on can be pinpointed and the whole season designed around them. These aims clearly have to correspond to the athlete's ability, as do any specific times that are set as either targets or goals.

LONG-TERM AIM

All training programmes incorporate a general, overall plan for the athlete's future development in the form of a pattern of steady progressions characterized by specific targets, which need to be achieved by particular dates. To reiterate: training programmes should consider the long-term development of the athlete in the context of the target times that must be achieved and the objectives that need to be met in future championships.

S.M.A.R.T.

When setting these aims or goals the coach should ensure that they are S.M.A.R.T. This means:

Specific – to the athlete's needs, abilities and requirements

Measurable – they can be measured, for instance, a set time achieved, a medal in a specific championship
Achievable – although challenging, the aims should be realistic and achievable
Relevant – the aims should be relevant to that particular athlete
Time-related – specific dates must be set by when the targets have to be achieved.

THE PLANNING REVIEW SHEET

When all of these points have been taken into consideration and evaluated, the coach and the athlete should then use a planning review sheet to establish the final aims and objectives. This ensures that the athlete's strengths and weaknesses from the previous season are highlighted. It also ensures that the correct qualities for the event are being covered, and that both the athlete and the coach commit their plan to paper so that it can be assessed and monitored, both throughout the season and at the end of the year. Below is an example of how to use the planning review sheet. It is a good idea to get the athlete to fill in his views of the season and bring his copy to the review meeting. You can see what his views are, the aims they have fulfilled and those that they have not, what his view is on his strengths and weaknesses regarding the event. Does he know what are the requirements of the event? What are the short- and the long-term goals, bearing in mind that they may be different from those of the coach? The following is a blank sample review sheet, which he can bring, filled in to the review meeting.

The following is a completed review sheet, which both the coach and the athlete have formulated together and agreed upon. This will include their joint views of the previous season and their aims, recommendations, refinements and targets for the forthcoming one.

PLANNING REVIEW SHEET

Name: Age:

Review of Season:

Aims:

Were the Aims Achieved?

Positive Points:

Areas Requiring Attention:

Requirement	Event Requirement	Athlete's Strengths
Speed		
Strength		
Endurance		
Power		
strength-endurance		
speed-endurance		
mental strength		
Mobility		
Technique		
Tactics		

Solutions to Areas Requiring Attention:

Regeneration:

Diet:

Warm Weather:

Race Requirements:

Aims: Short-Term:

Aims: Long-Term:

PLANNING REVIEW SHEET

Name: Julie Vaughan   **Age:** 24

Review of Season: 2005 – leading to the 2006 season.

Aims: 800m: 2min 2.5sec; 1,000m: 2min 34sec; 1,500m: 4min 5sec; 3,000m: 8min 50sec; win the National Championships 1,500m; gain selection for the World Championship team and achieve a personal best in the 1,500m final.

Were the Aims Achieved? 800m: 2min 2.2sec; 1,000m: 2min 33.6sec; 1,500m: 4min 7.9sec; 3,000m: 8min 54sec Won the National Championships, but did not achieve the qualifying standard for the World Championships.

Positive Points: Three of the aims met. The 3,000m event contested only once and therefore the aim could have been achieved. Speed showed a significant improvement. Strength-endurance improved – showed in being able to run three races in two days. Endurance improved – a much improved cross-country season and ability to cope with a higher mileage.

Areas Requiring Attention: Speed-endurance needs attention, particularly the longer repetitions – 500m/600m Tactics – need to be more versatile – other methods than leading only from the front.

Requirement	Event Requirement	Athlete's Strengths
Speed	★★★	★★★
strength	★★★	★★★
endurance	★★★	★★★
power	★★★	★★(★)
strength-endurance	★★★	★★★
Speed-endurance	★★★★	★★
mental strength	★★★★	★★
mobility	★★★★	★★★
technique	★★★★	★★★
tactics	★★★★	★★

Maximum rating: ★★★★★

Solutions to Areas Requiring Attention: Longer speed endurance repetitions Tactical training using split intervals, pace surges, alternating pace sessions. Early season low key races to experiment tactically and gain confidence. Look at undertaking an indoor season to be sharp for the Commonwealth Games in March.

PLANNING REVIEW SHEET (cont.)

Regeneration: Two weeks active break from running.

Full medical assessment – set up physiological testing dates for the next season.

Diet: Check weekly diet sheets – make recommendations on diet, supplements and vitamins, where applicable.

Warm Weather: Twice at specific times of the year – four weeks in March in Australia, prior to Commonwealth Games. When selected for European Championships – two weeks in Cyprus prior to Championships in August.

Race Requirements: 3 indoor races – 2 at 800m, 1 at 1,500m prior to the Commonwealth Games.
5 races prior to European Trials, comprising 1 × 3,000m, 2 × 800m, 2 × 1500m
After the trials: a fast Grand Prix 1,500m

Aims: Short Term: 800m: sub 2min; 1,500m: 4min 3sec; 3,000m: 8min 45sec
A medal in the Commonwealth Games, final of European Championships.

Aims: Long Term: 800m: 1min 58sec; 1,500m: 3min 57sec; 3000m: sub 8min 40sec
Medals at next Commonwealth/European and World Championships, Gold in Beijing in 2008

It is crucial that the coach ensures that the athlete makes progress throughout his athletic career and moves forward to the correct next stage at the correct time. The coach must also make sure that the athlete does not take any short cuts or miss out any key developmental qualities. The best maxim for the coach is to 'hurry slowly'. This means that he should not try to make the athlete accomplish his targets too quickly, for this will mean that the athlete fails to reach his full potential. Nor should the athlete do too much of any of the essential qualities required for his event, otherwise he will become overtrained and stale. Sometimes 'less is more'. This means that better results and benefits may be achieved by doing less training, but of the correct type and in the correct proportions.

Fig. 117 below shows how an athlete's training plan develops and progresses over time. The figures on progressions in training over a three-year period indicate how one athlete's training emphasis will change over this time. It may be seen from these examples that the emphasis in training has shifted from being primarily endurance-based to being speed-endurance based, with a greater emphasis on speed. This does not, however, deflect from the continuing consolidation of the athlete's endurance base.

Once all of the foregoing has been assessed and recorded, the coach and the athlete are in a position to start planning the yearly programme. This is sometimes referred to as periodization.

PERIODIZATION

In a periodized year, usually from October until the following September, the season is broken down into four distinct areas:

An 800/1,500 metre Runner

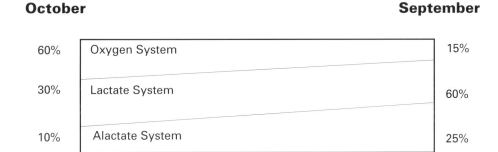

October **September**

75%	Oxygen System (Aerobic) H.R. 120 – 160	30%
20%	Lactate System (Anaerobic) H.R. 160 – 190	50%
5%	Sprinting / Bounding etc (Anaerobic – Alactate)	20%

Three Years Later

October **September**

60%	Oxygen System	15%
30%	Lactate System	60%
10%	Alactate System	25%

Fig.117. This figure shows how a young middle-distance runner will progress over a three-year period. Once he has built up a good aerobic-endurance base and reached maturation, he may then begin to slowly increase the anaerobic work he is capable of managing. In this way, as the training programme develops it also begins to change its emphasis.

a. Preparation phase – general conditioning (approximately November to January)
b. Adaptation phase – specific conditioning (January to May)
c. Application phase – competition training and competitions (approximately May to September)
d. Transition phase – recuperation, rest, recovery (October).

Within these four areas the year is then subdivided into the following phases:

• General base (endurance, strength, mobility, technique)
• Progressive development (the above plus strength-endurance, conditioning)

• Progression in intensity (including power, speed, speed-endurance) leading to low-level competition experience)
• Sharpening towards competitive climax
• Competitive climax
• Transition (recovery/rest phase, which may be either active or passive).

These types of periodization are illustrated in Fig.118 and 119. If the athlete is attempting a double periodized year, which requires two peaks – one for the indoor season and one for the outdoor one, or the Commonwealth Games in March and the European Championships in August, his periodized year is shown in Fig.120. A double periodized year can provide the potential for

Periodization

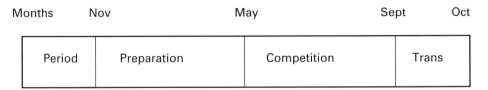

Fig.118. This shows the general breakdown of a periodized year into the three main periods of preparation, competition and transition.

Months	Nov		March	May	June	July	Aug	Sept	Oct
Phases	1		2	3	4	5		6	
Period	Preparation			Competition				Trans	

Fig.119. This figure shows how the three main periods of a periodized year are sub-divided again into the following phases: general preparation phase (1), specific preparation phase (2), pre-competition phase (3), competition phase (4), competition climax (5) and the transition phase (6).

Double Periodized Year

Months:	Nov:	Dec:	Jan:	Feb:	Mar:	Apr:	May	Jun:	July	Aug	Sep	Oct
Phases	1.1	2.1		3.1	1.2		2.2	3.2	4		5	6
	Preparation			Comp	Preparation		Comp				Trans	

Fig.120. In this figure the athlete is planning a double-periodized year, with the Commonwealth Games followed by the European Championships. In this situation the year is sub-divided as follows: preparation phase (1.1), specific preparation phase (2.1), competition phase (3.1), preparation phase (1.2), specific preparation phase (2.2), pre-competition phase (3.2), competition phase (4), competition climax (5) transition and phase (6).

a greater increase in the athlete's performance. However, athlete and coach have to decide whether these benefits, and the time spent on competition work, outweigh the loss of general and specific training time that this year would involve.

As indicated below, there are other methods, or overviews, of how to progress the athlete's training throughout the year.

The first is by Arthur Lydiard (*see* Fig. 121), the New Zealand coach, who used the method of block training throughout the year. During each block phase of training he always concluded with one week during which he reduced the total mileage involved as a recovery phase, before moving on to the next, higher level mileage block. He followed this large block of endurance training with

Lydiard Method

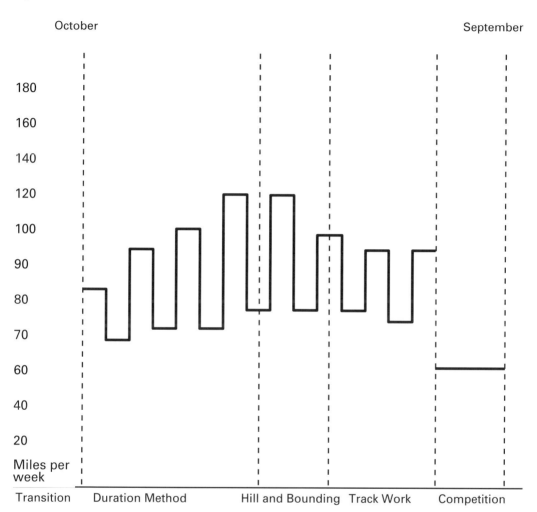

Fig.121. The Lydiard (block training method) is shown in this graph. During the duration period block of training, the volume increases each month, but there is a week of a smaller volume before each increase. The volume is maintained and then begins to decrease during the hill and bounding block of training. It decreases again during the track block of training, but still uses the monthly progressions, as in the other two blocks. In the competition phase the number of kilometres is at its lowest for the year and remains constant throughout.

blocks of hill repetition running and bounding. Lydiard then moved on to blocks of track work and downhill running before entering the final competition block. His last three blocks of training – hill running and bounding, track work and downhill running

and the competition block – all had far smaller mileages in the blocks than earlier in the year.

The second method is the Oregon method (*see* Fig. 122), sometimes called the Complex method, which was introduced at

The Oregon Method

Day	Week1	Week 2	Week 3	Week 4
Sunday	20 miles			
Monday	8 x 400(62) jog 400	10 x 400(62) jog 200	8 x 400(62) jog 100	10 x 400(62) jog 400
Tuesday	10 miles (alt)			
Wednesday	2(5 x 300) 46.5 jog 300/800	3(4 x 300) 46.5 jpg 200/800	4(3 x 300) 46.5 Jog 100/800	5(3 x 300) 46.5 jog 100/800
Thursday	60 mt *Fartlek*			
Friday	10 miles			
Saturday	Competition Cross Country			
	Indoor Time Trial etc			

Monthly Pace 62 sec for 400m. Next month 61 secs

Fig.122. The Oregon (complex) method of training has five days: Sunday – long run; Tuesday –10-mile run; Thursday – 1hr *fartlek*; Friday – 10-mile run; Saturday – competition or time trial. This remains constant throughout the monthly training cycle. The other two track sessions have a monthly goal pace (in this example 62sec). The Monday 400m session and the Wednesday 300m session are progressed to achieve the maximum number of repetitions with the minimum recovery at the set pace by the end of the month. If achieved, the goal pace is then changed for the following month.

the University of Oregon by Bill Bowerman. In this the key track sessions are on Mondays and Wednesdays, there are increases in the number of repetitions run over a four-week period and also reductions in recovery time, while the monthly pace-time set is retained; in this example 62sec for each 400m, progressing to 61sec for each 400m the following month. All other days remain the same, with a variety of long runs, steady-state runs, alternate-paced runs, fartlek and competition.

In Britain, coaches over the years have tended to use a mixture of training systems taken from other coaches from around the world. This led to the development of a system called the 'five-pace' system of training. This system encompasses over-distance track training, at 5,000m- and 3,000m-pace to improve endurance. It also involves under-distance track training at 800m- and 400m-pace to improve speed, as well as event-specific training at the specialist distance of 1,500m. Once the athlete can handle the repetitions and recoveries set out below, the recovery period is reduced until the original rest has been halved. Therefore over a period of six weeks the length and the number of repetitions would remain the same, but the recovery would be halved (for

Pace	Distance Jogged Recovery	Time of the Jog	Distance of Repetition	Training Day
5,000m	200m	1min	1 mile	Sunday
3,000m	300m	1min 30sec	1,200m	Tuesday
1,500m	400m	2min	800m	Thursday
800m	500m	2min 30sec	500m	Sunday
400m	400m	2min	200m	Tuesday

instance, 3 × 800m in 1min 50sec, with 2min recovery, will become six weeks later 3 × 800m in 1min 50 sec, with 1min recovery). When the rest time cannot be cut further, the original rest time is restored and the running time of the repetition reduced (example: 3 × 800m in 1min 47.5 sec, with 2min recovery). The development of the five-pace system is shown above; the times run in each repetition will be determined by the athlete's ability.

A woman with a personal best of 4min for 1,500m, therefore, would follow the following pattern of training, with the recovery times being slowly reduced until they are half the length of the original recovery time.

Sunday
5,000m pace: 3 × 1,500m in 4min 24sec, with 200m jog in 1min
Tuesday
3,000m pace: 3 × 1,200m in 3min 20sec with a 300m jog in 1min 30 sec
Thursday
1,500m pace: 3 × 800m in 2min 5sec with 400m jog in 2min
Sunday
800m pace: 3 × 500m in 70sec with a 500m jog in 2min 30sec
Tuesday
400m pace: 4 × 200m in 26sec with a 400m jog in 2min

None of these methods, however, will be successful unless the athlete has good time management skills. This is particularly important for one who has a full working day which involves travel, has a family, a social life and is also trying to fit in up to two training sessions in his already hectic and congested lifestyle. The high-performance middle-distance athlete needs as much recovery and rest time as possible. This is particularly the case if he is doing more than one session daily, and especially if they are intense sessions. The ideal situation for the high-performance athlete, particularly one with family commitments, would be for him to be either a full-time athlete or to work only part-time.

SUPPORT SYSTEMS

Support systems must be built into the planning and preparation work for any athlete, particularly as the athlete becomes more successful (*see* Fig. 31). These systems should be proactive, not reactive, and should be in place and utilized effectively and correctly to ensure that there are no injuries and that minor aches and problems are stopped at source. The list of support team members is important and potentially large, but not all may be employed or even necessary. It includes:

- Doctors: especially needed for blood tests, also crucial at key points of the season and when the athlete appears anaemic or stale.
- Masseurs: especially required after intense training sessions to get the athlete ready for the next session, and to identify any minor problems before they become major.

Fig.123. During the specific preparation phase the high-performance middle-distance runner may choose to test her endurance and aerobic base with an over-distance road race competition. Photo: Spencer G. Duval

Fig.124. To test his strength-endurance during the specific preparation phase the high-performance middle-distance runner may choose a muddy cross-country race. Photo: Spencer G. Duval

- Psychologist: if required, to ensure that the athlete is mentally strong and prepared for the racing season.
- Physiotherapist: to ensure that injuries are diagnosed and cured quickly.
- Strength conditioner: if the coach has no knowledge in this area, then this expert should be brought in.
- Funding/sponsor: crucial if the athlete is to maximize his potential and have a part-time job or be a full-time athlete.

RACE SELECTION

When planning a season the fixture list is crucial. This is so that predetermined races throughout the season can be included in the year's training plan. The races are carefully selected to help to gauge the athlete's fitness level during a particular training phase of the year. During the winter, if building up a good endurance base and improving the strength-endurance base have been the targets in the preparation phase of the season, he requires races to test them. The races could be an over-distance road race (*see* Fig. 123) to test endurance and a cross-country race in the mud to test strength-endurance (*see* Fig. 124). During

- Sports scientists: to do physiological testing, including blood lactate-level tests.
- Biomechanics specialist: to analyse the athlete's running action to ensure that it is efficient.
- Podiatrist: to provide orthotics (specialized insoles or supports) if recommended by the biomechanics specialist.
- Nutritionist: to ensure that the athlete has the correct food intake, a balanced diet and is taking the correct supplements.

the track season the coach and his athlete will have identified their race requirements in the build-up to the major race of the year. These requirements could include an early season over-distance race to test endurance, an under-distance race to test speed and as many other races as he feels that he may require, including the selection race to ensure that he is in peak condition for the major competition of the year.

EXTERNAL FACTORS

External factors will also play an important role in the total plan of a high-performance athlete, particularly if he is hoping to compete in major championships. Almost invariably, these championships will be held in hot or humid conditions. Therefore a certain amount of adaptation to heat and humidity in a similar climate should have been acquired before the championships. Other factors that could also affect the athlete are altitude, time change and the holding camp or the athletes' village.

Such factors can affect an athlete greatly when he is away from his normal training and living environment and when he is trying to taper his training so that he is in the peak of condition for the targeted race. The major problems that he will encounter if he is in a holding camp or an athletes' village are listed below. Thus plans and preparations to deal with these difficulties must be made before the athlete's arrival.

- Boredom: this may be a particular problem if the athlete is used to regular working and training; the question of how to fill the day becomes a difficulty and the major problem then becomes one of overtraining; this is caused by the athlete's trying to fill the available time with more training when, in fact, he should be easing down for the competition ahead.

- Group mentality: athletes can easily get sucked into inappropriate group-training sessions which are not beneficial for them, and in addition they may go on tiring sight-seeing visits when they should be resting.

- Loneliness: this is especially a problem if the athlete is away for a long time and has a family; to counter this difficulty a plentiful supply of books, music and other distractions need to be brought out to the camp or village.

- Food: athletes tend to either overeat or not eat enough, particularly if they are in a strange country; they need to be judicious in their choice and take cereals, energy bars and similar products with them.

- Massage: if not used to having a massage, the athlete should not have one before the competition because the body will not adjust to it; he should try it before he goes to the camp and then decide about massage.

- Training: with plenty of time being available, athletes can overtrain, train with a group or arrive without an individual plan; the athlete must have his own individual training schedule drawn up in conjunction with his coach and should follow this during his tapering period.

- Time zones: if there are time zones to cross and jet lag occurs, recovery days should be built into the training programme, with easy running being the order of the day; it takes approximately one day to recover from each hour of time change.

- Nerves: if the championship is a major one, athletes may become very nervous and have to ensure that they have enough to occupy themselves with in order to take their minds off the race.

- Atmosphere: a major championship stadium us, unlike other athletic meetings, may also have an adverse effect on competitors if they do not control their nerves effectively (see Fig. 125).

Fig.125. The competition target for the season is to perform with distinction at the major championships. The stadiums which host these championships have a unique and daunting atmosphere when full; the high-performance athlete needs to ensure that he can cope with this and not let it affect his nerves. Photo: Spencer G. Duval

- Hydration: it is imperative that athletes always have either a bottle of water or an isotonic drink with them to ensure that they are completely hydrated; they must constantly sip these fluids (*see* Fig. 126).

Fig.126. Whenever training at whatever time of year, the athlete should be constantly taking on fluids and hydrating. It is particularly important to do this at major championships in hot, humid weather and when training, at the warm-up track or post-competition by drinking water, or preferably isotonic, glucose and protein drinks if used in conjunction with refuelling. Photo: Spencer G. Duval

PLANNING THE PEAK

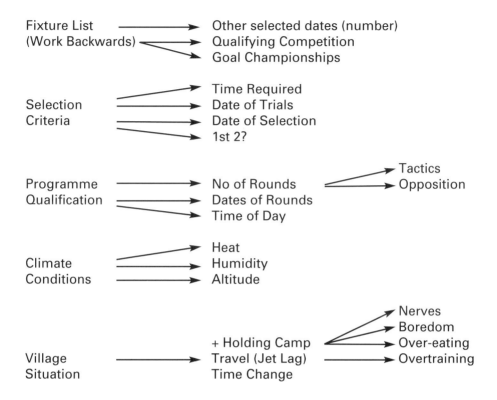

Fig.127. When planning the peak of the competitive season all the criteria detailed above must be taken into account. These include: the key race and selection dates, the selection criteria and qualification standards, the championship programme, the climatic conditions and the problems that may be encountered in a holding camp and/or competitors' village. All these points must be considered if the athlete is to arrive in his best condition with no distractions at the championships.

TAPERING

Tapering is the art of peaking for the targeted race of the year, whether it is a qualifying race or the championship race itself. The taper will start two to three weeks before the competition date. During this period the emphasis is on quality throughout (see Appendices). The taper has to be built into the athlete's training plan and should not be disrupted by the fact that he is at a holding camp or in an athletes' village. To ensure that the taper is effective the following must happen:

- the number of daily/weekly sessions should decrease
- strength work will only consolidate the work already done
- training will consist of mainly quality sessions and easy running
- the sessions will be light in order to retain energy and to keep the athlete fresh
- the sessions should also emphasize technique and relaxation
- the sessions will have few repetitions
- the recoveries will be long or complete
- the training sessions will be of high intensity

- the sessions should be carried out at race time
- these sessions will also keep the athlete mentally as well as physically sharp,

COMPETITION DAY

At a major athletic championships the athlete's whole day is geared to the competition and therefore everything else has to be planned backwards from the day and the competition race time. The athlete has to decide when he would want to start his warm-up, so that it finishes to coincide with the first call-up time. Once he has made this decision, he then has to decide at what time he wants to arrive at the warm-up track, before starting his warm-up. This will then determine what time he has to leave the athletes' village, taking into account the time it takes to get from it to the warm-up track. From this information he can then decide what is the optimum time for him to eat and relax before starting his journey to the track. Set out below is a typical schedule for an athlete at a major championship.

1:30 p.m.	lunch
2:15 p.m.	rest/pack kit into bag/mental preparation
3:30 p.m.	leave village and travel to warm-up track
4:00 p.m.	arrive warm-up track
4:30 p.m.	massage
5:00 p.m.	start warm-up
6:10 p.m.	call-up room 1, plenty of stretching
6:30 p.m.	call-up room 2, strides
6:45 p.m.	race
7:30 p.m.	cool down
8:00 p.m.	drugs test, plenty of hydration required
10:30 p.m.	return to camp/village
11:15 p.m.	eat

It is clear that planning and preparation are key if the athlete is to succeed and achieve his objectives during the season. Beginning with the reappraisal of the previous season, moving on to the transition period and continuing all the way through to the tapering phase and the competition day itself, everything has to be meticulously and methodically planned. Nothing should be left to chance. Everything that needs to be done should be carried out at the appropriate time and in the correct place to ensure that the aims for the season are met. An overview of what is required to plan for the athlete's yearly peak is shown in Fig. 127.

Remember: *if you fail to prepare, you prepare to fail.*

CHAPTER 7
Tactics

INTRODUCTION

Once all of the planning, preparation and training have been completed this must all be brought to fruition in the race. This means employing tactics to enable the athlete both to take full advantage of his strengths and to perform to his full ability. He has to have confidence in both himself and his preparation if he is to execute his tactics perfectly. The more successful the athlete becomes, the greater the possibility of his knowing little about his opposition. This is due to the fact that he will not have raced against this opposition as often as against his domestic opponents. Therefore self-knowledge and self-belief are the keys when preparing tactics for the race, the athlete, in conjunction with his coach, must ask himself the following questions before the final race plan is devised.

How fit am I? The answer to this will determine the tactics that he is able to employ. The fitter the athlete, the more involvement he will have in the race. If it is early season or he is just coming back from injury he may find it difficult to control the race as he would have done had he been fully fit. If the athlete is in the peak of condition he will be confident in being able not only to devise a race plan but also able to execute it effectively, and be prepared for any eventuality that may occur in the race. How important is the race to the athlete? Is it a minor event, a qualifying race, a heat or the target championship race of the season? Whatever the answer is will determine the

athlete's choice of race plan. What time of day is the event? In a major championship heats and qualifying rounds may be run in the early morning or the late evening and therefore the athlete should have prepared for this in his planning. Will the climatic conditions have an effect? Is it hot or humid? If so, the warm-up will have to be adjusted accordingly, the correct kit worn and the athlete should ensure that he has a continuous intake of fluids.

These points are intended to give the athlete every opportunity to execute his race plan effectively. If every eventuality has not been correctly covered the race plan is likely to fail. Hot or humid conditions will mean that it is not as easy to be a front runner and so alternatives must be planned. Has the athlete travelled through one or more time zones en route to the event? If so, the correct amount of time should have been allowed for the athlete to adjust and be back to running normally. A lack of focus and alertness brought about by jet lag could ruin any race plan. Is the race at altitude? If so, the tactics employed should allow for the race to be run at as economical a pace as possible. Is it cold, wet or windy? Any of these factors could affect the plan for the race, and particularly if it is windy since it is energy-sapping to lead into the wind – it is far better to shelter behind the opposition until the chosen time to attack. Once all these variables have been taken into account the athlete should consider the ways in which he could run the race. The following are the main tactical ways:

METHODS OF RUNNING A RACE

Short Sprint

Whether the race is run at a fast or a slow pace, the athlete employing a short sprint finish will not attack and take the lead until the final 100m, or even closer to the finish. This type of runner is known as either a 'kicker' or a 'waiter'; this means that he will wait until the last possible moment to attack, making it difficult for the opposition to respond to his attack. This type of finish not only requires a good basic speed, but also the ability to accelerate quickly.

Long Sprint

Here the athlete who is not so strong in a short sprint finish will attack from much further out in the race. This is likely to occur at between 300 and 400m from the finish line. The idea of the long sprint is to nullify the effect of the short sprint finisher, making it difficult for him to use his normal race tactics successfully. To do this the runner has to position himself in the correct place at the correct time, and ensure that there are no other athletes in the way to obstruct his long run for the finish. But once committed, he must keep going at full pace. If he fails to do this he will allow the sprinters to hang on and get past him in the finishing straight.

Building up the Pace

Athletes who have neither a particularly good short nor long sprint finish would adopt this race tactic. In a 1,500m race the athlete employing these tactics would take over the lead with 500 to 600m of the race remaining. From here he would ensure that the pace got progressively quicker over each successive 100m. With this tactic he would hope to nullify the finish of both the long and the short sprint finisher, or at least get rid of most of them before the finish. This tactic requires not only good strength-endurance but also good pace judgement and great self-confidence. Again, once committed, the athlete must carry on increasing the pace or his rivals will hang on to him and potentially be able to launch their own short sprint finishes.

Lead throughout the Race

An athlete who lacks much basic speed or finds it difficult to accelerate will make little or no impact in a sprint finish. Whether it is a long or a short sprint finish, the runner who is so lacking should look for an alternative tactical plan. One method is to lead from the front of the field, making it a hard pace throughout the race, from gun to tape. This type of tactic has three main advantages: first, it ensures that the race is not slow and therefore will not play into the hands of the sprint finishers, secondly, when it comes to the sprint finish it puts everyone on a more equal footing than it would have been in a slowly run race, and finally, because the athlete is in the lead, he can dictate the pace, have an uncluttered run throughout the race, run the shortest route and not be caught up in the physical contact of the pack. However, if it is windy, hot or humid, this is a difficult way to run the race and it needs a strong athlete to be able to execute these tactics successfully. The athlete employing these tactics should have confidence in his own ability to run this way, since it will become apparent only in the closing stages of the race whether the tactical plan has been effective enough and has eroded the sprint of the fast-finishing runners. If the athlete is not at the peak of fitness he would be wise not to attempt this tactic.

Mixing up the Pace

Another tactical method, particularly for an athlete who lacks a good sprint finish but does not mind leading throughout the race, is to mix up the pace. This method of constantly surging faster to increase the pace and then slowing the pace, only to increase it yet again, upsets the rhythm of the following athletes. Athletes like to run at a constant pace and not have this pace disrupted. Therefore not only is the pace of the following athletes disrupted, it also saps their energy and their confidence as they try to conserve energy for a sprint finish. This tactic requires great strength-endurance, speed-endurance as well as great self-belief.

Attacking in the Middle of the Race

For someone without a fast finish who does not like to lead throughout, this is an excellent tactical method to use. However, it needs an athlete strong both physically and mentally to adopt it. There is always a point in the race where athletes consciously or sub-consciously relax and run slower than in other parts in an attempt to save energy for the finish. In an 800m race this is usually between the 200 and the 600m point, and in a mile race it will invariably be in the third lap. Therefore this is where the athlete employing this method would attack. He will run this part of the race much faster than would be expected to ensure that the other athletes suffer physically and are also taken by surprise. This should get rid of most of the opposition, desirably creating a gap over the chasing athletes and negating the finishing effect of either the short or the long sprint finishers.

Even Pace Running

This is particularly relevant to the 800m race because of the large proportion of anaerobic involvement in the event. With this particular tactic, therefore, the aim is to maintain both efficiency and economy of effort throughout the race by running each of the two laps in as similar a time as possible. While this tactic is recommended by the experts, it is followed by only a few world-class 800m runners (Yuriy Borzakovskiy, the Athens Olympic 800m champion, is an excellent example). Most 800m races tend to have faster first-lap times, for which the athlete must be prepared both physically and mentally. The 800m race where the second lap is faster than the first, referred to as 'negative splits', is not as common a tactic as the faster first lap. However, this type of race may become very tactical and comes down, not only to who is the fastest finisher but who is in the correct place at the correct time in the race to execute his finish.

The athlete must now consider taking everything into account to decide which of these methods he will employ.

THE CHOSEN TACTICAL APPROACH

However, there are certain other aspects which have to be taken into account before the athlete decides which of the race strategies he is going to adopt. He must consider what his strengths and weaknesses are and adapt both his training and race plan to accommodate them. He must also decide how fit he is at this particular time of the season, for the fitter he is, the greater his confidence and the more flexible his race strategy can be. He must take into account how good his pace judgement is and his ability to accelerate. These are aspects that he should have highlighted as part of his training throughout the build-up phase. During this he should have also worked on his ability to relax, particularly when fatigued, and how to distribute his economy of effort. The weather too will play a part in which tactical approach to choose.

How well he measures up to these demands and how well his training has gone will give him the required confidence for the forthcoming race and aid his tactical selection. However, before making his tactical decision there is one more important point to take into account – if this information is known: who are the main opposition and what are their main strengths and weaknesses?

THE OPPOSITION

If the opposition is known, the coach and the athlete will be able to work out their strengths and weaknesses. It is also likely that their preferred method of racing will be known. When considering the opposition's strengths, weaknesses and preferred racing method, one factor which must be taken into consideration is whether this method would be sustainable through three or four rounds of championship competition. It is also wise to consider which runners dislike being in a pack, physical contact and the constant jostling that this involves. Who prefers to lead and is easily discouraged if they lose the lead position? Who would not relish either a long, hard run or a long sprint finish? Who is good in paced grand prix races but finds it difficult in slowly run tactical races? Who crowds the leader, clips their heels and tries to upset the leader's rhythm and concentration? Who is strong, or weak, mentally when the pressure is on? Who prefers a slow pace because he has a very strong short sprint finish? Who, for example, would find the call room at major championships, where he is held for 20min in two different rooms in close proximity to the opposition a daunting and strength-sapping experience?

While these questions are not as important as those the athlete has asked himself, they will have a bearing on the chosen tactical approach to the race. In a major championship, taking into account the varying opposition from round to round, it is quite conceivable that the athlete will have to adopt three or four different plans, depending on the number of rounds in the competition.

THE RACE

Once the athlete has taken into consideration his own ability, whether he is racing for a time or racing to win, the ability of the opposition, the weather, the race's importance and the qualifying conditions, he must formulate his tactical plan. He must decide where he preferably would like to be positioned in the early stages of the race and the best position to be in relation to the leaders. However, he needs to ensure that he does not get boxed in (*see* Fig. 128) and is in the correct position where he has decided he will make his attack. This is on the shoulder of the race leader, or about 1m further back (*see* Fig. 129). This allows him to be free from any physical contact, and in this position he can respond quickly to any sudden changes of pace ahead of him and react to any changes or attacks that may come from behind. He is also blocking off the runners behind him and they will have to run wide if they wish to overtake him, giving him time to respond to them. He must ensure that he is focused and concentrating at all times and is ready to anticipate any sudden move or attack by the opposition. If he becomes boxed in he must not panic but wait for a slight gap to appear, quickly fill it and then move from this position into the one he wants to be in. It is inadvisable for him to slow and let others pass him so that he can then move back round the outside of the field. If he tries to slow down and go round the back of the other runners the pace may have increased and he will be left even further behind. He must also ensure, particularly if the race is being run at a fast pace, that he does not attack on the crown of the bend (*see* Fig. 130) and waste valuable time and energy. The 800m race is akin to physical chess and therefore it is advisable, where possible, to avoid undue physical contact. He must remain

800 – Coming to the Bell

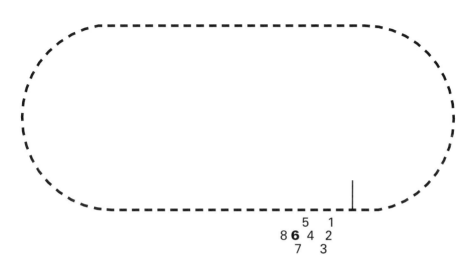

Fig.128. In this figure the eight athletes are coming to the bell for the last lap in an 800m race. Number 1 has the pole position, with number 2 running abreast and number 3, to avoid losing contact, is running unwisely wide with the bend approaching. Number 7 will have to run wide to improve his position, as will number 8. This means that numbers 4, 5 and particularly 6 are boxed and will be even more so if numbers 7 and 8 do move up alongside them. They will either have to wait for the back straight before they extricate themselves, for a gap to appear or have to come out and waste energy running wide around the bend. If it has been a relative slow first lap and one of numbers 1, 2 or 3 accelerates quickly, the athletes in the box, and particularly number 6, will be unable to respond, possibly not until the back straight when it will be too late.

calm in this situation since invariably, as athletes turn into the home straight, they will drift wide and spread across the first few lanes of the finishing straight. This usually leaves spaces through which the athlete can take the shortest possible route to the tape (*see* Fig. 131).

Above all, in a tight, tense race the athlete must keep his cool and not panic nor become taut. He must be aware at all times of what is happening around him, repeat what he has been doing repeatedly in training – maintain his technique, keep relaxed and keep driving towards the tape. If he tenses up his technique and running speed are likely to deteriorate. He must run right through the tape to ensure that he is not passed as he eases off short of the finishing line. Once he makes his effort he

should focus on the finishing line and never look back. Above all he must be flexible, have a contingency plan and be able to think on his feet in the middle of the race. This means being proactive, not reactive, to any situations that may occur in case the race does not develop as he expects it to and he cannot put his tactical plan into operation. If this does happen, he must remain calm and focused, then he will be able to react positively to this new situation. He must develop a racing instinct.

RACE PREPARATION

There are certain types of training that should be included in the athlete's programme to help him prepare for the many

1,500m – Last Lap

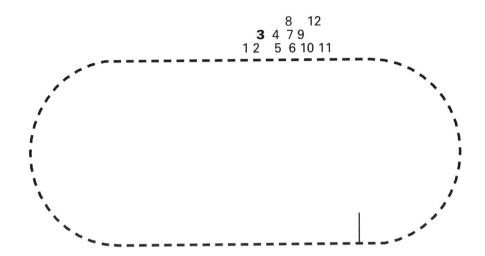

Fig.129. This figure shows the field still together with 260m left to run in a 1,500m race. Runner number 3 is in the pole position to dictate what happens in the latter part of the race. He is ideally positioned, just off the leader's shoulder, to respond to any change of pace and with number 2 trapped on the inside. He is also in a position to be able to react to any athlete coming up on his outside. With the bend approaching quickly, any athlete who wishes to pass number 3 will have to run wide all round the bend and waste valuable energy as the finish approaches.

800m – Passing on a Bend – Last Lap

Fig.130. As this 800m race approaches the finishing straight, numbers 4 and 5 are having to run exceedingly wide, hence wasting energy to stay in touch with the leaders. Having had to run hard and wide all the way round the bend at a fast pace will not leave them in the best physical shape for the long sprint finish down the home straight. Their position may be made even worse if number 2 moves up to the leader, which will have the effect of making them have to run even wider still. The shortest route is always a straight line.

1,500m – Finishing Straight

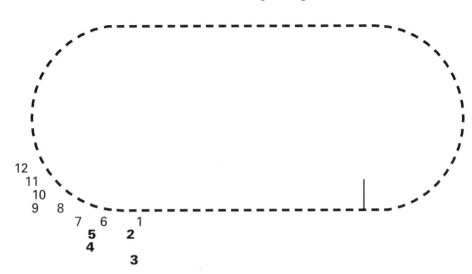

Fig.131. This shows a 1,500m race coming into the finishing straight. What tends to happen, particularly in championship races, is that several of the runners will drift wide as they come off the final bend. Some do this consciously in their search for a better position and a free uncluttered run to the line, others do not realize that they are doing it. In this figure numbers 2, 3, 4 and 5 have all to varying degrees drifted wide as they come off the final bend. What the other runners need to do, unlike in the previous figure, is run as close to the inside as possible. This, however, takes courage, but they can be assured that, as the runners in front begin to drift outwards as they come off the bend, gaps will appear for them to come through. Remember that the finishing straight is 100m long and much can happen during that distance, so do not panic!

variables in race running. He should work constantly on relaxation and his technique since these are the first elements that deteriorate under pressure and fatigue. He must learn in training how to float when running quickly; this means being able to run quickly in a relaxed way without overexertion and while maintaining his technique. This allows him to adopt a sprint finish at the end of a fast-run race. Speed is a key element in any race, whether it is deployed from a long way out, throughout the race or in the finishing straight. Therefore the speed sessions covered earlier in this book should be an important part of any training programme; these should include acceleration sprints over distances ranging from 60 to 300m, skills sprinting, drills, downhill sprints, reaction drills, differentials, group running, running with a following wind, over distance repetitions, speed-endurance sessions and event-specific sessions.

To decide which tactics to employ, therefore, is not a simple matter since many variables have to be considered. These include the athlete's own strengths and weaknesses, and above all his own self-confidence in addition to the strengths and weaknesses of the opposition and the tactical method that they prefer. The time of year, the importance of the race and the weather will all have a bearing on the final tactical decision. If the runner is in the peak of condition and believes in himself, he will have the confidence to choose the correct plan for the race and the weather. Such a plan will complement his ability but also be flexible enough to counter any eventuality that may occur in the race.

APPENDIX
Training Schedules

1. FOR A HIGH-PERFORMANCE MALE, 800M RUNNER

The following four schedules are for the specific preparation phase, pre-competition phase, competition phase and tapering phase for a 24-year-old male 800m runner with a personal best of 1min 45sec; he has been training for 12 years. The training schedules are based on twelve sessions per week (micro-cycle) and are for four different weeks (micro-cycles) of the year.

Training percentage levels:

intervals	100
tempo run	95
long run	90
steady run	85
recovery run	75

The distances run each week do not include warm-up and cool-down distances. The athlete, in addition to the training programme, would be doing daily mobility and core stability exercises. The intervals are all run at a 100 per cent effort, applicable to his fitness at the specific time of the year. The only exception is that, during the competition and the tapering phase of the season, the intervals are event-specific, which means that target times are relevant to the speed required to achieve the athlete's seasonal target time.

Male 800m: Specific Preparation Phase, Late March; 120km per Week		
Day	a.m.	p.m.
Sunday	drills, strides and acceleration; sprints 6 × 150m, complete recovery (marathon > sprint pace)	long run 20–25km
Monday	steady 12km	Oregon circuit + 30min recovery run
Tuesday	drills, strides + steady 12km	12km alternating pace run or 12km tempo run
Wednesday	recovery run 10km	steady 12km run
Thursday	plyometrics + hill training; 2 × (4 × 200m) jog back recovery/4min between sets; 30min recovery run	weight training session + 10km steady run
Friday	rest	rest + massage
Saturday	skill sprints (4 × 4 × 60m, walk back recovery + 3min between sets) + 6 × 1,200m on grass with 1min 30sec recovery	30min recovery run or 45min aerobic pool work

Male 800m: Pre-Competition Phase, Early May; 100km per Week

Day	a.m.	p.m.
Sunday	drills, strides and acceleration; sprints + 30min steady run	long run 20–25km
Monday	steady 12km run	gym circuit training + 30min recovery run
Tuesday	steady 12km run	track session: 2 × 600m with 15min recovery + 5 × 300m with 4min recovery between repetitions
Wednesday	30min recovery run	steady 12km run
Thursday	3 × 30m/40m/50m/60m/70m/80m. 2min between sprints and 10min between sets	weight training session
Friday	rest	rest + massage
Saturday	track session: 3 × (500m/300m) with 30sec between repetitions and 8min between sets	30min recovery run or 45min aerobic pool work

Male 800m: Competition Phase, Late June; 80km per Week

Day	a.m.	p.m.
Sunday	long 20km run	
Monday	steady 12km run	45min *fartlek*, 12 bursts: 1,000m to 80m
Tuesday	30min recovery run	track session at race pace: 200m/500m/100m; recovery: 20sec/20sec/10min 4 × 200m with 4min recovery
Wednesday	steady 10km run	drills, strides + steady 10km run
Thursday	track session: 4 × (5 × 40m) with 2min recovery and 6min between sets.	reduced weight training session
Friday	rest	rest + massage
Saturday	7 × 150m sprints with a complete recovery between repetitions	30min recovery run

Male 800m: Tapering Phase, Late August; 65km per Week		
Day	a.m.	p.m.
Sunday	long run 18–20km	rest
Monday	drills, strides + steady 10km run	track session: one set at race pace, 300m/300m/200m with 20sec/10sec recovery
Tuesday	30min recovery run	reduced weight training session
Wednesday	steady 10km run	track session: 3 × 3 × 50m with 2min between repetitions and 6min between sets
Thursday	30min recovery run	drills + strides
Friday	Track × 300m at race pace simulation + 20min recovery run	massage
Saturday	easy 15min jog + strides	target competition of the year

2. FOR A HIGH-PERFORMANCE FEMALE, 1,500M RUNNER

The following schedules are for a 28-year-old female 1,500m runner with a personal best of 3min 58sec who has been training for 13 years. The four micro-cycles are based on twelve sessions per micro-cycle week and cover a micro-cycle for the specific preparation phase, the pre-competition phase, the competition phase and the tapering phase for the target competition of the year. The same criteria apply as for the male 800m runner with regard to training level percentages, warm-up and cool-down and daily mobility and core stability.

Female 1,500m: Specific Preparation Phase, Late March; 140km per Week		
Day	*a.m.*	*p.m.*
Sunday	long run 25km	drills, strides + 10k run
Monday	steady 12km run	weight training session + steady 10km run
Tuesday	steady 15km run	1 hour *fartlek* – with 12 bursts – 1,200m to 60m
Wednesday	30min recovery run	gym circuit training + 30min steady run
Thursday	steady 15km run	hill training 5 × 300m with jog back recovery + 30min recovery run
Friday	steady 12km run	30min recovery run
Saturday	drills, sprints + grass session of 8 × 1,000m with a recovery run of 1min 30sec	rest + massage

Female 1,500m: Pre-competition Phase, Mid May; 120km per Week		
Day	*a.m.*	*p.m.*
Sunday	long run 25km	drills + acceleration sprints of 6 150m with 3min recovery + 30min recovery run
Monday	steady 12km run	weight training session + steady 10km run
Tuesday	steady 12km run	track session: 2 × 1,000m with 10min recovery + 3 × 200m with 4min recovery
Wednesday	30min recovery run	drills, strides + steady 12km run
Thursday	acceleration sprints: 5 × (3 × 40m) with 2min and 8min recovery + 30min steady run	circuit training session
Friday	steady 10km run	rest + massage
Saturday	track session: 2 × (3 × 500m) with 1min 30sec and 8min recovery	30min recovery run

Female 1,500m: Competition Phase, Late June; 100km per Week

Day	a.m.	p.m.
Sunday	long run 25km	drills + 4 sets of skills sprints 4 × (3 × 60m); recovery 2min and 8min
Monday	steady 12km run	reduced weight training session + steady 10km run
Tuesday	steady 12km run	track session at race pace: 500m/700m/300m 30sec recovery + 5 × 300m, with 1min recovery
Wednesday	30min recovery run	strides + steady 10km run
Thursday	5 × 60m/50m/40m/30m/20m; recovery: 2min/8min + 30min recovery run	steady 10km run
Friday	rest	rest + hydrotherapy
Saturday	track session at race pace: 2 × (1,000m/400m); recovery jog 100m/12min recovery	30min recovery run

Female 1,500m: Taper Week, Late August; 75km per Week

Day	a.m.	p.m.
Sunday	long run 18km	acceleration sprints: 6 × 50m. 3min recovery (marathon > sprint pace)
Monday	steady 10km run	reduced weight training session
Tuesday	30min recovery run	track session at race pace: 500m/400m/300m/200m/100m with 40sec/30sec/20sec/10sec recovery
Wednesday	30min recovery run	steady 10km run
Thursday	3 × (3 × 50m) recovery: 3min/8min + 30min recovery run	steady 10km
Friday	race simulation 1 × 500m at race pace + 20min jog	rest + hydrotherapy
Saturday	rest + massage	target competition for year

3. FOR A HIGH-PERFORMANCE FEMALE, JUNIOR 800M RUNNER AND A CLUB-STANDARD MALE 1,500M RUNNER

The following two micro-cycles are for a young female 800m runner and a male 1,500m club runner.

The first micro-cycle is for the pre-competition phase for a 17-year-old female who trains five times per week. She has a personal best of 2min 12.1sec and has been training for four years.

Young Female 800m: Pre-Competition Period, Late May; 50km per Week		
Day	*a.m.*	*p.m.*
Sunday	long run 15km + strides	
Monday		speed-endurance track session: 2 × (600m/200m) (100sec/33sec) with 1min/8min recovery + strides
Tuesday		circuit + 10km run
Wednesday		speed track session; 3 × (4 × 50m) with 2min/5min recovery + easy 8km recovery run
Thursday		drills + steady 12km
Friday		rest
Saturday		race

The following micro-cycle is for the specific preparation phase for a male club 1,500m runner with a personal best of 3min 44.9sec and who has been running for ten years and trains seven times a week.

Male Club 1,500m: Specific Preparation Period, Early April; 70km per Week		
Day	*a.m.*	*p.m.*
Sunday		long run 20km
Monday		strides and steady 10km run
Tuesday		speed endurance track session: (3 × 500m) (72secs) 3min recovery; 10min jog and then (4 × 300m) (45sec) with 1min recovery
Wednesday		weights + steady 12km
Thursday		speed track session: 6 × 150m acceleration runs 4min recovery + easy 10km run
Friday		rest
Saturday	steady 12km run	grass session: drills + 6 × 1,000m with 90sec recovery

4. FOR AN INTERNATIONAL MALE STEEPLECHASER

Two micro-cycles for a 27-year-old international steeplechaser with a personal best of 8min 21.5sec; he has been running for 14 years, 5 specializing at the steeplechase event; he is able to fit in twelve training sessions per week, including three early morning runs. The two micro-cycles are for the preparation phase during mid November and the competition phase during early July. All the technique work is done over hurdles, not barriers.

Male Steeplechaser: Preparation Phase, Mid October; 120km per Week		
Day	*a.m.*	*p.m.*
Sunday	technique work/drills using hurdles	long run 30km
Monday		general conditioning circuit + steady 12km
Tuesday	steady 10km run	6 × 1,000m on the road with 2min recovery + drills + steady 10km
Wednesday	steady 10km	steady 15km
Thursday	steady 10km	1hr *fartlek* – 15 bursts, 1,200m/60min
Friday		rest
Saturday	strength endurance track session: 10 × 400m in 66sec, with 1min recovery including 3 hurdles	30min recovery run

Male Steeplechaser: Competition Phase, Mid July; 85km per Week		
Day	*a.m.*	*p.m.*
Sunday	technique/drills using hurdles	long run 20km
Monday		reduced weight session + steady 12km
Tuesday	steady 10km run	Speed endurance track session: 3 × (800m/200m) (2min 5sec/30sec) (30sec/8min recovery) 10min jog (4 × 300m) (45sec) (2min recovery)
Wednesday	steady 10km	steady 10km
Thursday	steady 10km	speed track session: acceleration runs 2 × (6 × 150m) (3min/6min recovery) + easy 20min run
Friday		rest
Saturday	event specific track session: 3 × 1,000m (2min 45sec) (1min 30sec recovery) with 5 hurdles	30min recovery run

Glossary

Adenosine diphosphate (ADP) high-energy phosphate compound from which ATP is formed.

Adenosine triphosphate (ATP) high-energy phosphate compound from which the body derives energy.

Aerobic energy pathway involving the oxygen transportation system and the use of oxygen in the mitochondria of the working muscle for the oxidation of glycogen or fatty acids.

Agonist working a muscle in the direction of movement.

Alactate anaerobic system the name often used for the energy pathway involving the cycle of ATP being broken down into ADP and recycled by phosphates.

Anabolism the building of body tissue, the constructive phase of metabolism.

Anaerobic in the absence of oxygen.

Antagonist one muscle counteracting the action of another; for instance, along with agonist muscles working against each other on opposite sides of a joint.

ATP-PC system a simple anaerobic energy system that functions to maintain ATP levels: the breakdown of creatine phosphate frees phosphate which then combines with ADP to form ATP.

Basal metabolism energy output of the entire body necessary for the maintenance of life and performance.

Biomechanics the study of the human body and movement in sport.

Catabolism the tearing down of body tissue.

Concentric action muscle shortening.

Creatine phosphate (CP) energy-rich compound that plays a vital role in providing energy for muscle action by maintaining the ATP concentration.

Dehydration loss of body fluids.

Eccentric action muscle lengthening.

Erogenic aid a substance or phenomenon which may improve athletic performance.

Erythropietin the hormone which stimulates red blood cell production.

Fast-twitch fibres (FT) a muscle type with low oxidative capacity and a high glycolytic capacity; associated with speed or power activities.

Gluconeogenesis conversion of fat or protein into glucose.

Glucose a carbohydrate and the principal supplier of energy during muscular work.

Glycogen the storage form of carbohydrate in the body, found predominantly in the muscles and liver.

Glycogenesis conversion of glucose to glycogen.

Glycolytic system system that produces energy through glycolysis.

Haemoglobin iron-containing pigment in red blood cells that binds oxygen.

Homeostasis – the stability of the life process.

Hormone chemical substance produced or released by an endocrine gland and transported by the blood to a specific target tissue.

Intracellular fluid the approximate 60–65 per cent of total body water contained in the cells.

Lactic acid substance produced in the body during the initial phase of work and heavy exercise.

Lactate threshold the point during exercise of increasing intensity at which blood lactate begins to accumulate rapidly above resting levels.

Maximum volume up-take (Max VO2) maximal capacity for oxygen consumption by the body during maximal exercise; oxygen uptake is the difference in oxygen content between the air inspired and that expired, also referred to as aerobic power, maximal oxygen consumption or cardio-respiratory endurance capacity.

Metabolic reserves bodily reserves called upon in periods of special need; a decrease in these is a sign of health problems or functional defect.

Muscular endurance ability of a muscle to avoid fatigue.

Muscle fibre individual muscle cell.

Myocardium muscles of the heart.

Macro-cycle the number of meso-cycles forming a major part of an overall training plan for a year.

Meso-cycle group of micro-cycles designed to gain maximum benefit at a particular phase of the season.

Micro-cycle an organized group of units to provide an optimum training value for each unit.

Nerve impulse electrical signal conducted along a neuron; can be transmitted to another neuron or a group of muscle fibres.

Neuromuscular junction site at which a motor neuron communicates with a muscle fibre

OBLA onset of blood lactate accumulation.

Orthotic used in running shoes and spikes to keep the body's balance when there is a problem with running technique.

Overload progressive heightening of intensity in training to ensure that there is a higher level of adaptation in the body.

Oxidative system most complex energy system in the body, generating a high energy yield by breaking down fuel with the aid of oxygen.

Oxygen debt total oxygen uptake after exercise minus initial resting oxygen uptake.

Oxygen transport system components of the cardiovascular and respiratory systems involved in the transporting of oxygen.

Podiatrist in conjunction with a biomechanical expert, provides orthotics for running shoe or spikes to correct any imbalance in running technique.

Plyometrics series of ballet-type exercises involving single-, alternate- and double-footed hopping and/or skipping to improve the power and strength at speed of an athlete.

Pronation anti-clockwise movement of a limb.

Reversibility when intensity, extent or density levels are reduced in training, the achieved level of bodily adaptation will gradually weaken.

Slow twitch fibre (ST) type of muscle fibre with a high oxidative and a low glycolitic capacity; associated with endurance-type activities.

Specificity the physiological adaptation in response to intense training is specific to the training activity; to ensure maximum benefit the training should be relevant to the individual athlete's performance requirements.

Speed-endurance type of training designed to ensure that the athlete does not slow down when running at maximum speed, particularly when energy is produced predominantly through the anaerobic breakdown of glucose (lactic-energy production).

Supination clockwise movement of a limb.

Bibliography

F.W. Dick, *Sports Training Principles* (A. & C. Black, 2003)

IAAF, *Level II Advanced Coaching Theory Textbook* (2003)

D.E. Martin and P.N. Coe, *Training Distance Runners* (Leisure Press, 1991)

H. Wilson, *Running My Way* (Sackville Press, 1988)

Index